SUE CAMPBELL

TWO BRICKS SHORT

MY JOURNEY WITH CANCER

ILLUSTRATED BY WAYNE WRIGHT

Complete cataloguing record for this book may be obtained from the National Library's online database at www.collectionscanada.ca/amicus/index-e.html

warning: THIS BOOK MAY CONTAIN
Fragmented thoughts from ASSORTED NUTS

Published by Changing Tides, Summerside PEI
changingtides@outlook.com

Part of the profits from the sale of this book will be donated to the Palliative Care Unit of the Prince County Hospital, Summerside, PEI

ISBN: 978-0-9937846-0-6 (sc)
ISBN: 978-1-4834-2022-6 (e)

Rev. date: 11/6/2014

DEDICATION

This book is dedicated to my precious sister, Vicki who went to be an angel on October 15, 2008, leaving all the pain and anguish of cancer behind her to go to a place where there is no pain, only love.

and to:

My youngest sister Tishy who's suffering has just begun. May she place all of our faith, hope and prayers into her heart and soul so that she stays strong and wins the battle.

- to all those who have suffered and gone before us, God bless you all!

"And with each generation, so our souls live on and on, and our lives and all of our pain is therefore worthwhile." Ralph Waldo Emerson

TWO BRICKS SHORT,
MY JOURNEY WITH CANCER
SUE CAMPBELL

mailto:changtides@outlook.com

ACKNOWLEDGEMENTS: I want to thank Wayne Wright who encouraged me to continue writing and then to finish this book - and for drawing all of the brilliant illustrations. To my children, Steve and Janice, who drove me, supported me and held my hand through the most scary moments of my life; Janice, God love her who had a fund raiser and bingo for me. Grandma Mac for all her love and support and for letting me win at least one game of crib. To the Campbell family and all who supported me with money, prayers, help and phone calls. Neighbours who helped me with grass cutting and snow shoveling, thank you. To all of the doctors and nurses in oncology units all across the world, God Bless you! Sue

FOREWORD:

When a person, any person is diagnosed with cancer, it hits like a ton of bricks. Instant emotional thought: OMG I am going to die. I am too young to die, please no, not me!

Personally I have always been two bricks short of a load, and taking that into consideration, I refused to accept a death sentence, and I certainly wasn't afraid to go headlong into battle. Going headlong into battle is much easier for me, you see there is very little in my head to go into battle with.

I was wondering if a person were two bricks short, how many would be left in the load? I called my good friend Faye and asked her how many bricks were in a load. We worked together for years at the same building supply company in downtown Summerside and I knew she would laugh, but eventually find an answer for me. She asked Angela, another old friend who answered "there are five hundred bricks per pallet. They would weigh about 2500 pounds, 500 pounds over a ton and that would be a load" What a girl.

Cancer strikes fear into everyone. It is a horrible disease and the family, friends, partners and all others in the life of the sufferer are affected and hurt for that beloved person who has been struck by such a cruel disease that puts fear right into their heart and soul.

A year before my diagnosis with lung cancer and our excursions across to Halifax, my son Steve had his own battle with cancer. When he first told me, I cried and asked God "why?"

"I told Steven that he was young with a wife and three kids in high school, if I could, I would take this cancer from him and suffer it for him myself." He said "Why would you say that, Mom?" I answered "You are young, you have three beautiful kids to raise, I am old, it is something that I would do for you if I could".

Steve has always been the best man a person could ever know. Loving husband, the best Dad in the world, great son, and friend who has given his shirt to so many. How could this be happening? He had surgery in Charlottetown and went through several rounds of chemo. Then, not a year had passed when I was diagnosed. Steve has been in complete remission.

We all pray that someday soon there will be a cure and in the meantime we must keep putting one foot ahead of the other, keep a smile on our faces and pray that it can be beaten thanking God for each new day.

Now, I feel so much bliss in living. Poking my head out of the door on a cold winter morning, breathing in, tasting, and just feeling a new day. I look out to the side of the driveway and see only a foot of my trees poking out of the snow. The wonder of nature is that there are little leaf buds all along the tiny fragile branches, and life goes on.

Being two bricks short has helped my attitude and makes me think of a print at Community Connections, a day programme and residential and work placement for people with disabilities here in Summerside it tells us, and I quote:

"Our lives are determined not by what life brings to us, or demands of us, which may at times be cruel, but by the attitude *we* bring to our lives. It is a catalyst, a spark that starts a spark in others to more and more people who pass on that feeling of positive attitude in their lives." – my old friend Author Unknown

I will live each day to the fullest with or without hair and thank God that I am ONE HOT GRANDMA!

Sue Campbell
Photo I.D.

CHAPTER ONE

Just to Live
You have to believe that life will go on
with or without you.
You have to be able to reach out and
talk to someone, tell someone
that you are hurting and needing.
You need to have courage and know
that you can face each challenge
and greet each dawn with a smile and
a prayer and you need to laugh and cry
and have unshakeable faith and courage
- believing that your spring will come,
like the faith and courage of a crocus
that is blooming in the snow.
Sue

In October of 2012, I was re-diagnosed with cancer in my left lung, that was when I decided, not that life had dealt me a lousy hand, but if I stayed strong and played that hand betting my life against the odds, determined to win, even more determined that I would beat it, and that is what I vowed to do!

Yes, I have been afraid, I have cried, cursed, been depressed, but I am still strong, like a tea bag, I don't show how strong I am until I'm in hot water. I really felt that after my third cancer surgery which was an upper left lung lobectomy, that I would have beaten the damn disease. Actually, I went through the surgery like a seasoned trooper. Of course, without coming across as a full of faith and hope bragging bitch, with an I told you so attitude, two years later the attitude has changed, now it is " please dear God, enough is enough, I really don't want to die."

The first time, the rotten "C word" came was in the fall of 1989. It reared its ugly head as a lump in my right breast. I went in for needle biopsy where a needle was inserted into the tumor and fluid from inside the tumor was then sent to the lab for analysis. The oncologist decided that I needed surgery. The pathology report reported a ductal carcinoma in situ. For the first time in my life, I was facing the fact that perhaps life was a bad joke which could be and may be very short. I had to have a talk with myself: I said, "Listen, self, at the age of forty-four, you are much too smart, too good looking and way too young to die." There now, nothing wrong with my ego. So when the surgeon explained that the tumour had been self-contained and that "he is certain he got it all", and "it had not spread". I said "thank you God", feeling very humbled and relieved.

I was admitted to the hospital the day before surgery at exactly two o'clock, or I imagined that my bed would be given to another, (probably a younger, better looking patient,) and I couldn't have that! I was in a room with a

2

gal who was into her second surgery she had one breast removed and now it had now the cancer was back up in the other. We chatted away and after supper we went to see a movie about breast cancer surgery. Back in the room, we talked away about our families and life in general. Around nine that night, in came a nurse and gave us each a sedative. We wished each other good luck and slept quite well, ready for the next morning. At seven a.m. I was taken down in a wheel chair to mammography where they would do "mapping and markings" on my breast to show exactly where the tumour was and where the surgeon should be cutting. After the big squeeze, I was pushed out into the hall and left there. What I thought was at least an hour had passed. I told a passing nurse that I had been scheduled for surgery that morning and could she please look into that. I couldn't help it, I started crying. Sure enough, they had taken other patients in before me which meant another wait. Oh well, two days later, I went home with a large plastic cup and layers of bandage over my breast to hold it up with a huge amount of tape. No, I am not bragging or saying that my boobs were ever that big, but they did used to be perky and cute. So started my one ugly tit syndrome.

There was, of course a chance that it might return, however, chances were excellent that with this type of tumour, it would not.

Again, I thanked God after all, I had all the best parts of life ahead of me - - like seeing my kids grow up and marry, becoming a grandmother, and maybe even finding a man with whom I had more than one thing in common.

So, I recovered quickly, and went back to work, plus keeping house, mothering and growing Swiss chard in between the roses and petunias. Time went by and other than having an ugly right boob, no one would ever guess. I had good intentions with the Swiss chard, but forgot what it looked like and exactly where I planted it, so when it disappeared, I figured that I had probably pulled it for weeds. My sister Vicki would have said "That's our Susie, great at dreaming, but not too bright in the real world, two bricks short, y'know."

Back then, what feels like the middle ages, mammography was booked by the physician and only if the doctor suspected a problem. It had been about five years since the surgery and my doctor booked me for a mamo.

There was a long waiting list at the time, so he marked the requisition "Semi-urgent," which meant that I had to be put forward, toward the front of the list.

The appointment date arrived and while waiting, at the old Prince County Hospital, the gal, young and good looking, who was booking the appointments, told me "You are lucky to get in this soon, the waiting list is huge and some will have to wait for months". This made me feel a bit guilty, however this mamo, thank God, turned out clear.

Then, in 2000, the mammo scan showed a small irregularity, again in the right breast. I wasn't quite as scared, but you never know, do you? The second one could be the killer, cancer can be sneaky and deceitful. Even a change in a small tumour can be more deadly and spread faster than a biggy.

My family doctor set up an appointment with the surgeon who would be doing the biopsy. I saw him in his office, and no matter how much I tried to joke about cancer he never once cracked a smile - - - instead, he told me what would he happening during the surgery. Apparently, I would be getting a "needle biopsy" which I thought was a matter of the doctor inserting a needle into my breast and withdrawing fluid, which would then be tested and determine if the tumour was cancer or not. I had that procedure before my first breast surgery, ten years before. Apparently that type of biopsy was not what I would be getting. Now a needle biopsy meant that a radiologist from the mammogram department would look at my breast image on a screen and insert several needles to pinpoint the tumour to be biopsied. On my way out, the surgeon's assistant gave me a date for the surgery, telling me to show up at the hospital in "day surgery" at 7:30 a.m., as I would be first in.

I arrived on time, filled in my forms, put on one of those sexy blue gowns, (that give you no comfort if you are freezing cold like I am most of the time) and waited in the breast screening department for them to pin point the tumour. The radiologist was running away behind that day and so I had to sit there freezing and waiting. Finally he squished my poor boob in the mammo machine and inserted several needles which, I would say were each about four inches long. After they were all inserted, he told me NOT to move and stay there still squished until he could look at the pictures and determine if we needed more needles. Examination could take a little time as he was running late. After what I thought was a lot of time, I started crying again. To me, having to wait with my poor ugly boob squished in the machine meant there was something badly wrong. To me, the hardest part about cancer is not knowing. Not necessarily so, apparently, the man could have been called out to another patient, or even taken a fast run up to Tim's for a coffee, who knows. He finally returned and told me not to move my right arm or any part of my body that would move the needles, or the whole process would have to be done again. Then he left me on a bed in the day surgery holding area.

Several hours later, my mouth had dried out. I had been fasting since the night before and had thought that I was first in. Of course the anxiety was killing me, I would have given anything for a cup of coffee, or a small glass of juice. The nurse brought me a tiny container of water and an ice cube. She was very kind, explaining that there couldn't be anything in my tummy or I might regurgitate during the surgery. Biopsy surgery is one thing, but waiting and waiting and waiting with caffeine withdrawals was really hard on the head. I knew the surgeon was behind because I had to wait for the radiologist so I guess I was put down to then end of the list. Why? I didn't have a clue - maybe he didn't like the look of my one ugly tit, but I had many regrets over trying to make him laugh. I learned later from a nurse "that is just his way".

Almost crazy on a skinny surgery bed with every nerve and muscle taunt so that I wouldn't move or move any of the long needles that precariously poked out of my breast played hell with my sanity. I was so stiff and tense

˙ . . . I started thinking maybe he had run up to
Tim's for a coffee who knows.

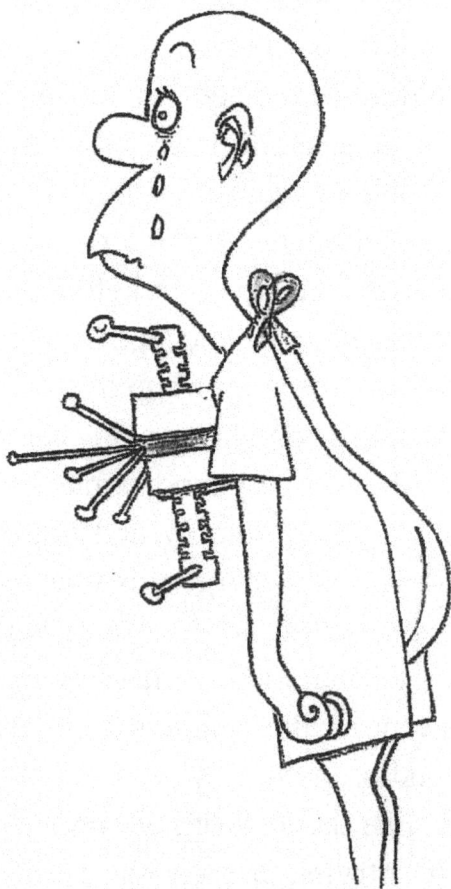

that by the time they wheeled me into the OR, I was into major distress, so frustrated and angry that I was crying again. You know . . . those tears that run silently from you eyes and down into your hair behind the ears - yeah that kind, the ones that say, " hey, I am feeling sorry for myself here, does anybody care?" It's not you that has the lump along with six or so long needles sticking out of your weird looking boob; that has every muscle in your body cramping and aching from not moving for several hours and doesn't even have a man to sit there with, hold her hand, or go home to - - but, think on this one girl. O.K., I thought on it - forget the man. They shot something into my IV line that put me into La La Land. When I woke up, a nurse was checking my dressing and of course, I asked her what the results of the biopsy were. She told me that the surgeon would be in to discuss this very soon. The day surgery had been packed full that morning shortly after I checked in, now there was only me.

The promise of "very soon" turned out to be another hour or so. By that time I had decided that the surgeon didn't want to tell me the bad news. After a couple of serious panic attacks, I began planning my funeral. Well sir, I had picked the nicest hymns and readings and I was ready to start crying again. So, when he finally came in and told me that it was not cancer I was so relieved, but I had to cancel the whole damned funeral thing, hymns and all, and the worst of it was that my right boob was even uglier.

After a couple of serious panic attacks, I began planning my funeral.

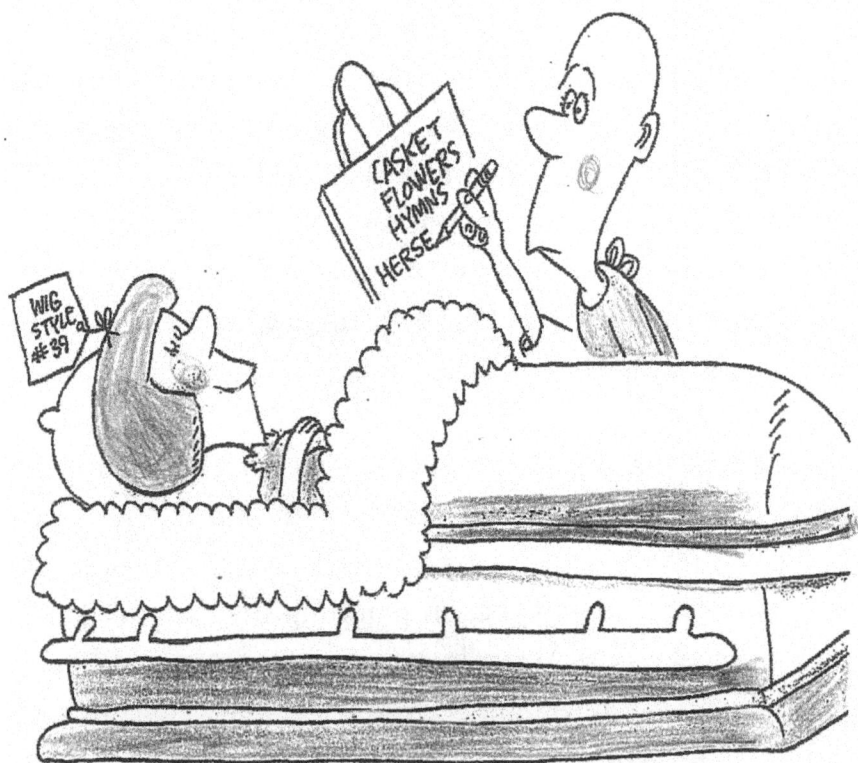

CHAPTER TWO

GRANDMA'S JOY

I look into your eyes and feel the joy
of knowing that you are part of me
and knowing that I am now
worthwhile and complete.
His plan has always been
that our souls live on in the lives
of our children and their children.
Now I feel, that special
connection with the Universe
and with my heart full of pride and love,
I know that my purpose in life
has gone full circle and been completed
so that when I am gone,
part of me will stay with you forever.

Years passed and life went on. There were good times
and hard times, Steve and Janice were married and had three
beautiful children, but alas, no Prince Charming and thank
God, no more cancer. So, I decided that if Prince Charming
wants to find me, he will, but no way am I looking for him.

In the summer on the Island, we all have lots of visitors and in 2010, we had more than lots, family and friends from near and far. We spent some lovely fun days and nights together picking up shore treasures, barbecuing and partying. I hadn't been feeling great and tired easily but tried very hard not to let it show. I had been getting short of breath with pain under my ribs and sharp pain if I bent over, I had no idea the rotten old cancer was hiding, no, waiting, looming in the shadows.

I was not quite sick, but always tired and lethargic (my excuse for leaving the housework for another day) with aches and pains in my muscles and bones and lower rib pain that was not agonizing, but there, nevertheless. I kept seeing my family doctor, Dr. Paul Kelly who is the kindest and most caring person on earth, and I think at this point, we were both praying it would all go away. Dr. K. also thought, this was a mystery disease and admitted that he didn't know the cause. For starters, he sent me for a chest x-ray, and very quickly thereafter for a CT- scan.

I knew something was really badly wrong as Dr. Kelly called me himself and asked if I could come into his office the following day. My son, Steve came with me to hold my hand just in case, and sure enough, there it was, a lovely, well formed rather large tumor in the upper lobe of my left lung, my heart was pounding. As this is a very small Island, oncologists and specialized surgeons are not plentiful. Doctor Kelly told me that I had been referred to the QE2 in Halifax firstly for a PET- scan, which by definition would show any cancer in my body and therefore eliminate the need for a surgical biopsy. He had reviewed and reported on the images and referred me to a surgeon in Halifax at the Cancer Clinic at QE2. He agreed that the cancer in the upper lobe of my left lung could be removed successfully by surgery.

Weeks went by waiting for the first appointment and, of course, my mind had me imagining the tumor growing to a monster size, crawling up my throat and choking me. I started planning the funeral again.

Damn, don't you just hate when that happens, I had forgotten the hymns I had chosen before, so had to start over.

Finally the call came in for a PET scan which, after an IV injection was to show every cancer and "iffy area" in my entire body. I was not to eat and was to drink lots of water prior to. It was cold and windy with snow flurries, so the four hour drive was not pleasant, not only for me, but also for my son who was driving and missing work.

I tried to sing in tune with the radio, but after Steve turned the station a few times and gave me some sideways glances, I got the silent message -- 'would you shut up, for God sake.' We wound around the streets of downtown Halifax and then realized that the buildings in front of us *were* the hospital.

QE2 in Halifax is HUGE! It was amazing how quickly we found the check-in for PET radiology about five minutes before the appointment time. I needed to pee so bad, I mean so bad that I was praying. Across the hall, hidden behind a door was relief, a washroom. I peed on and on and on and then went back to the check- in where my son had been doing a fine job giving all my facts. Good job too, I have an

... I had imagined the tumour growing to a monster size and crawling up my throat to choke me.

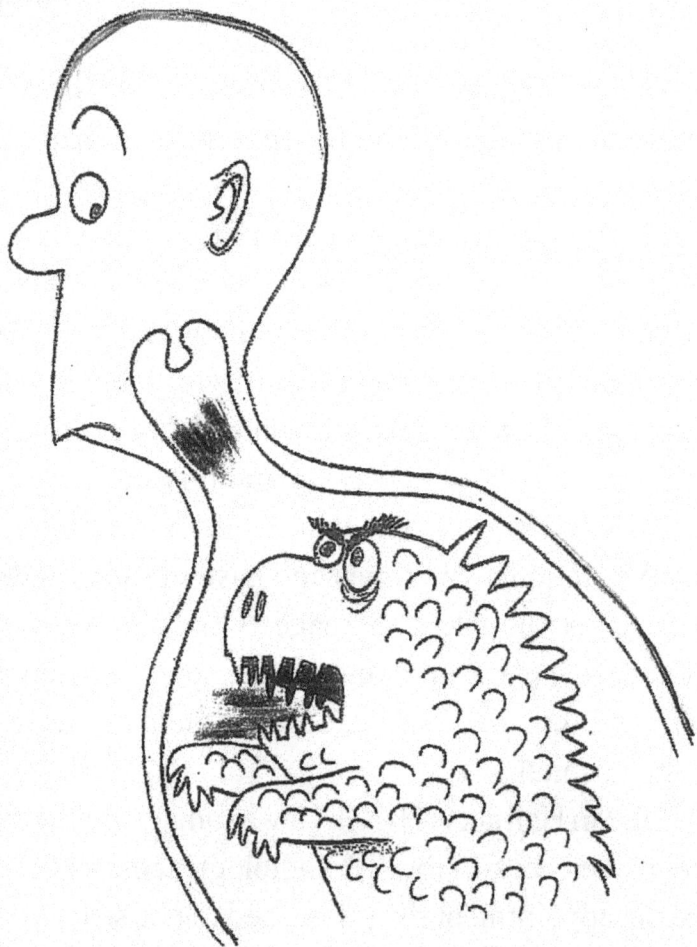

excellent memory except when it comes to important stuff. Once all the information had been collected, in came the nurse to collect some blood and the urine sample, HELLO! O.K. then, there was not a drop of pee to be given at least not right now. She told me not to worry, the check was for drugs and alcohol, you don't look as if you have been on either. No, but I wish. A couple of shots of shine might do me good right now!

Steve and I sat in the PET waiting room and chatted with another couple from the Island also waiting when a lady in a lab coat came out of the inner sanctum and told us that the serum that was to be injected into us prior to our PET scan had been dropped on the floor by the junior tech and we would have to be re-scheduled. JUST LOVELY, wonderful. Away we went to drive four hours home, not a cheerful drive, no, I didn't try singing again. My son was chewing on a few choice words, actually, so was I. When I was young, I forbid myself to say curse words even in my head, but boys oh boys, I have aged since then!

About three weeks later along came another appointment. This time we knew where to go and what to do. Away we went. Typical East Coast November weather, cold and wet with on and off snow. It's funny, when you are on a four hour road trip with someone who had to lose a day's pay, and just does not want to be there, the more a person tries to make the driver smile, the harder he tries to be pleasant, all in all, it was pretty uneventful, but awful.

We arrived in lots of time for me to have a short visit to the washroom and still drink the rest of the water, at least enough for a test. I went into the machine for about twenty

In came a nurse to collect blood and a urine sample but there was not a drop to be given.

minutes, actually, they ask each patient if claustrophobia is a problem. While I was in there, I wondered what they did if the answer was yes. I slid into a machine no bigger around than a driveway culvert with my arms up and cramping over my head was no picnic. I reminded myself to quit bitching as this scan had saved many, many lives and that could include mine. I watched the numbers count down just above my face and so the scan was completed. My arms were cramped stiff, but what a brave girl I was. I was hoping for a pat on the back, or at least a lollipop, but no such luck. On the way home, I told Steve that I deserved a cheeseburger, so wake me up when he spotted the golden arches. I knew deep down that I should stay awake and keep him company, but as soon as he told me to put the seat back and close my eyes, I was "outta there, gonzo."

Back home full of anticipation and a few days later, I spoke to one of the nurses at the medical clinic and asked her for a copy of my PET scan report. I had no idea if I could make sense of it, but dammit, I am the one with cancer. She told me it was in and she would photo copy it and leave a copy at the front desk. In I went on the dead run and came back home with an envelope containing my life or death. I dialed the phone as I opened the envelope and read out loud the contents of the report to my son and daughter -in- law, who of course, along with every other tech device on the planet have a speaker phone - I, being just a little older still remember the old crank phone on the farm. The scan showed a definite tumor in the upper part of my left lung and reported other areas of concern in of several lymph node sites and one up in my neck. On page three, it showed a totally different type of lung cancer, different type, different symptoms.

My daughter-in-law said "this is not good". I didn't have a clue what was good or not good. At this point, I knew that cancer was not good and I wanted it gone out of my life. My daughter in law, Janice had recently lost a close friend to cancer which I guessed by this time was really bad. I re-read the entire report before I got on the computer to find out what was going on. Sometimes you have the to trust the Internet to tell the truth. Google, who I in general consider one of my best friends (don't ever quote me on that) with regard to stuff that I don't understand will usually come up with an answer and anyone two bricks short needs good friends. I may have to click a few times but eventually it will always come up with some kind of an explanation. The computer report was even worse than the one that I had conjured up in my imagination.

Then I noticed that on each of page one and two of the report, there were my identifications of health card number and date of birth. Then on page three there was a card number and date of birth that were *not* mine. O.K., people, let's just scare the shit out me. I called my doctor's office and spoke again with the nurse. She was genuinely horrified. " Oh, God, I am so, so sorry!" The fax from Halifax came in with both reports. The receiving assistant, by accident, photo copied the report(s) and stapled them together. I had received not only my report, but also the report of another patient, and she too was " So sorry!" (Deep breath), me too. My family had me dead already. Not me, I am not near ready to die, I have too much to do, too much shit to raise and too many things to accomplish.

On page three, there was a Medical Records
Number and date of birth that were not mine!

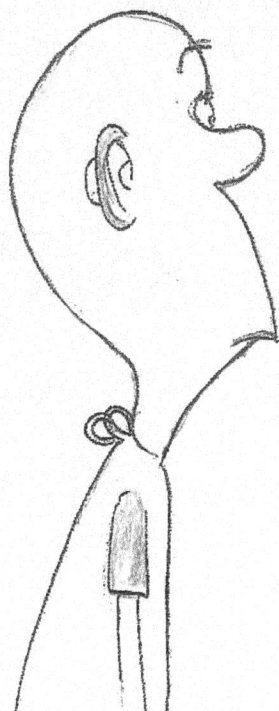

One of the hardest parts about having cancer is waiting. It is like waiting for a balloon to burst, or for the boss to start yelling at you, especially as you know that every day you wait, the tumor is trying to grow and spread. Anyway, let's move past the anxiety of waiting and move on to the surgery without passing Go, or . .

That was in November. Now, in the first week in February, I finally get a call to attend in Halifax for a meeting with the surgeon. Away go Steve and I again in the four wheel drive pickup in cold slippery weather, but bright sunshine. On the way over, I can see little trees along the side of the road that look like baby birch trees. I tell Steve I want him to stop and dig some for me to take home for my back yard against the fence, going on to explain that at this time of year they would transplant well and I could just picture them up the yard.

"Yeah, right, Mom, we are on our way to see the surgeon that will operate on your lung so you won't die and you want me to stop the damned truck and dig up baby trees? Sorry, Mom, maybe next time."

"Awww why?" (I am really quite good at whining to get my own way -).

"To tell the truth, Mom, for some reason, I didn't think to bring a bucket, a spade or an ice pick for the frozen solid February ground, remind me next time."

We met with the surgeon who told us that he would try to remove the tumour by laparoscopic surgery. He explained that it would involve two small incisions plus another even smaller for a drainage tube. He would release the tumour and pull it out through a tube all the while watching what he was doing by way of a laparoscopic camera inside another tube. This would be the least invasive form of surgery and that his assistant would call with an appointment. He didn't know at this point if I would require follow up chemo or radiation, it would depend on the pathology report after the surgery.

On the way home I still looked longingly at the little birch trees, but soon the darkness took over my longing, and I fell asleep.

Back at home, life went on. I was working full-time, as a care-giver to three mentally disabled adults in my home. That in itself is a very demanding and 24/7 job. I had already looked into who would care for them during and after my surgery. I downplayed the cancer to them as they would not fully understand, but I did tell them that I wasn't feeling the very best. I would have to go to Halifax for a while and they would be going to their respite workers until I was feeling better and then they would be coming home.

I got a call from a lady who told me that she was one of the liaison nurses who worked co-ordinating patients between QE2 in Halifax and the Island, to make sure that I would be well taken care of. If I had any questions, I could ask her now or I could call any time and if they didn't answer, to leave a message. I called a few days later and spoke to the same lady. I was inquiring about care at home after my return from Halifax. She told me that she would be at QE2 after my surgery, to see that all went well and would arrange for home-care before I came back to Summerside, so that I wouldn't have to spend time traveling to the hospital for incision care. The home care nurse would

... we are on our way to see a surgeon that
will operate on your lung and save your life
and you want me to stop the damned
truck and dig up baby trees???

YOU ARE
NOW LEAVING
THE
BABY TREES
HAVE A NICE DAY

make sure my vitals were good and I would be helped with my shower and personal care. This made me feel more comfortable and confident.

A call from the QE2 Cancer Unit told me that because of the location of the tumour within the lung, the laparoscopic surgery could not be performed as planned. I would need full surgery including removal of a rib or two, after all what is a couple of ribs when three quarters of your lung is coming out? A large incision would be made from just under the back shoulder blade down to past the bottom of the rib cage. I had been referred to a different surgeon who would need to see me the next week.

Away we went again, my son and I in the four wheel drive truck. Is this getting a bit monotonous? I didn't even look at the cute little trees on the side of the road. Was I pissed off? Yes, oh, yes! My son had to lose pay driving me over and I had to pay for gas and Bridge tolls for all these trips. I had no money, when you don't work, you don't get a pay check.

As a care-giver for mentally disabled adults, I was paid by the government as a contractor and had no sick days, EI, CP, pension plan, medical/dental, seniority, or any other benefit. I had no-one to answer questions, the rules were simple, I was considered an independent contractor and had to fend for myself. So, when a person gets a diagnosis of cancer, or any other serious disease, that person, (especially if there is no partner to support her) is alone financially, emotionally and in every other way. There is no where to go, I was financially on my own and people that were in my care had to be taken care of by approved respite providers.

Pay for respite runs about double the amount that the caregiver gets and is payable by the day. Each respite provider had to agree to the amount per day offered by the Disability division of Social Services. If I had not enough respite hours built up for such an illness, then I had to pay the difference, or give up that client to be cared for by someone else. For me, this meant little or no income for now or in the future. I felt destitute.

My DSP (Disability Support) worker and my home care worker were very kind, helpful and sympathetic. So was I.

It wasn't only the cancer that I had to deal with, it was also, how the hell could I support myself? How could I pay for the drugs I needed and any special supports?

In the last week of February, 2011, Steve drove me over to Halifax to check me into QE2 for cancer surgery and have the upper lobe (about two thirds) of my left lung removed. We checked into the hospital and they told us that I needed to be ready for surgery the next morning at 7:30 AM.

On the way over, there was no longing for baby trees, I didn't even ask for a cheeseburger and neither of us was in a joking mood.

We checked into the "Lodge", which is a hotel type building, only a block and a half from the QE2 where people from outside Halifax could stay for a reasonable rate, which is good! There is almost no parking there and no parking on the street, so the only other option is the hospital overnight parking lot, and pay for it. That is where the truck was parked for the next couple of days.

Steve and I went to the cafeteria for supper. I didn't eat much and after our meal, we went up to the room. My "other mother" Jean, her friend Joan and Jean's son all came up see me before the big event. I was not feeling the very best, (could be I was scared shitless) so as soon as I could, I said "Good night" and hit the sack, reminding Steve that we had to be up early in the morning.

To tell the truth, I hardly slept at all, just dozed off and on all night having dreams about climbing out of the window and escaping.

The hospital was only a few blocks away, but Steve insisted that he walk up to the hospital parking lot, get the truck and drive me. O.K. then, (love you).

We went up the elevator to the sixth floor and right across from the elevator was the check-in desk. The nurses did all their pre-surgery forms. One question was "Is there any possibility that you are pregnant"? I answered, "Well, I just might be, after all, I am only sixty five, haven't had a partner for sixteen years, but you never know what possibilities are, I am a born again virgin." I had blood tests, heart monitor, and God knows what else.

They hooked up an IV, gowned me, took my jewelry, and put my teeth into a Ziploc bag. (Ooops I didn't want to admit to false teeth, oh well, too late now). I kissed my son "Bye for now, love you" and they wheeled my bed into a waiting area. I know all about waiting areas from previous surgeries.

In the bed to my right, there was a man also from the Island. We chatted for a few minutes and he told me that it was in both of his lungs, the right one was coming

. . . well, I could be pregnant, I am only 65, and live alone, but I am a born again virgin.

out which would leave a small tumour in the left, so he was praying for miracles, after surgery, he was looking forward to at least a year of treatments. He had two kids, twelve and seven and his wife worked at a seasonal job. He sounded depressed or, at least negative, and down in the dumps so I tried to cheer him up. I told him there are miracles and that he had to believe, have faith and hope to get through this. The nurse put an injection into his IV line and said "You all set, Terry?" "Yep, lets go!" I wished him luck.

"See ya" he said and they wheeled his bed out.

It wasn't long before the team came in, hung another bag on my IV stand, injected it and asked, "You all set, Sue"? I didn't even answer, the injection knocked me out cold.

When I started to come around, I was in "post op" along with several other post op patients. Steve was sitting beside the bed holding my hand. I was half way in and half way out of a dream so I told Steve in a weak and whispering voice, "see that nurse over there, well she shot me!"

"Oh no," he laughed, "did it hurt?" - - back to the dream. When I came around again, probably hours later, Steve was still there, right beside me, still holding my hand. I was much more with it. I told him that he shouldn't stay here and watch me sleep and to go home to his family. " Don't worry, I will call you when I can come home." Don't ask me how long later, but I half opened my eyes. My hand was still on the side of the bed, his hand was gone, maybe out for a bite to eat, maybe gone home.

I slept for most of the next morning. When I woke, I was in a different room, all by myself. I had no-one to torture with my constant babble, so went back to sleep. The physio lady came in shortly after noon and re-hooked my tubes to an IV cart and helped me push it out to the hall, where I turned around and came back to bed. I amazed myself, "I strong like bull"! I told her. The physio lady just laughed and replied - "well, maybe wait and see".

The nurses were giving me morphine on a pretty regular basis and I was allowed to buzz them when *my* buzz wore off. The next day, a male nurse came in. During the morning I had examined the parts of my body that I could see and reported to him that my right arm was very badly bruised.

Then he reported back to me that when I first came in for surgery, after I was out cold, he hung me by the right arm on a large meat hook that hung on a railing from the ceiling and when they called my name, he gave me a push down the rail and into surgery I went. We both laughed, and finally he told me that I had been given blood thinners which caused the bruising.

"What about the fella?" I asked, "you know the one you pushed down the line ahead of me".

"To tell the truth, I wasn't working that day, do you remember his name?"

"Yes, he is an Islander, his name is Terry".

"Well then, I will find out and take you to see him if you want."

"Yes, that would be great, thanks!"

After about twenty minutes, he came back. He walked in shaking his head and I just knew.

. . . he hung me by the right arm on a meat hook and when they called my name, he pushed me down the rail and into surgery I went.

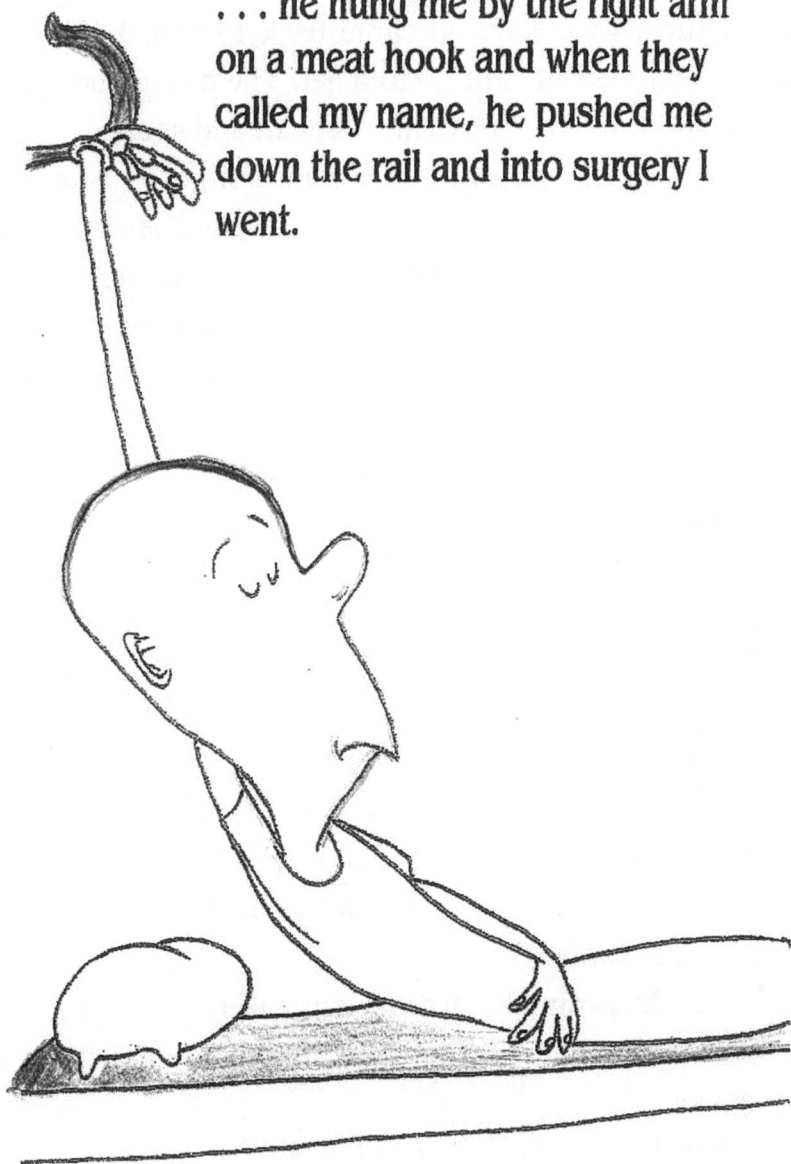

"Terry didn't make it. He bled out during surgery. I'm sorry, did you know him? In severe cases, depending on where the tumor is, it happens sometimes, but think of it, you are alive and *you* will make it."

I cried thinking of his wife and children and how horrible and ruthless this disease is.

Then, I had to smarten up, in came my doctor along with five or six interns doing their daily rounds. I told the doctor that I was as good as I could possibly be at my age without makeup, and asked him if he was sure that they didn't give me a frontal lobe lobotomy instead of an upper lobe lobectomy. Nobody laughed. O.K. - - fail, I tried.

On day three after surgery I began feeling down. Depression is something with which I am quite familiar and over the years I have become an expert at self-diagnosis. Feeling depressed apparently is quite common after major surgery. Feeling trapped isn't hard to figure as I had tubes in and out of every opening in my body. Hey, c'mon it's not like this is my first picnic. I glanced around the room to make sure no one was looking, I buried my face in the pillow and screamed, not too loud of course, I couldn't even think of bothering anyone and, for the second time in the whole ordeal, I cried. I was propped on the wrong side to reach the box of Kleenex on the bedside table. Again, looking around to see that no-one was watching, I pulled the side of my night-shirt up, blew my nose and wiped my eyes. There now, that felt better. Still sniffling, I fell asleep.

That nagging cramp that I thought was a fart couldn't be trusted. I decided best to press the button for a nurse. A few minutes passed and no-one came. The cramping

I asked if I had a frontal lobe lobotomy instead of an upper lobe lobectomy, nobody laughed.

moved further down. When it started rumbling, I knew I was in trouble. Oh, God, please don't let me shit the bed. I pressed again and again and finally tried to get out of bed by myself. As soon as my feet hit the floor, what was to be a fart splattered all over the place, down my legs, into my slippers, the wall, bed and everything within three feet was covered in shit.

There is a difference between crap, poop, and shit. Yes, they are all four letter words, but "holy crap" has now replaced "thank you" in the vocabulary of teenaged kids when they find a fifty in a birthday card. Poop is different, it is what you refer to when you first get the cute little furry puppy home, take her outside to the designated spot, and say "Make a poop for mommy - oh what a good little girl, that is such a cute little poop." Shit is different again, it is what you find six months later on the living room carpet and you scream, "You rotten dog, how dare you shit on the rug?" See the difference? The nurse never did come in. A couple of minutes after the splatter bomb dropped, I could see a cleaning lady outside my room, mopping the hall. I called her, she came in and wasn't hugely happy, but told me "after all, this is my chosen profession." She cleaned up, re-made the bed, hooked all the tubes back back from the cart to the stand, helped me with a wash down, into a clean shirt and back into bed. I was so-o-o ashamed and kept telling her how sorry I was. I thought she would say it was O.K. and forgive me, but she just gave me a "yea, right" look. I cried again until I fell asleep and dreamed about meeting up with Brad Pitt and for sure that will take the sting out of splattering shit all over one's room. Somehow that doesn't

. . .that nagging cramp I thought was a fart couldn't be trusted!

sound right, but what the heck this is my story. The next day I was up and walking again. The physio lady came in and hung all my tubes and stuff on the IV cart and away we went out into the hall, down as far as the elevator and back to bed. Next day we went further in the morning and in the afternoon she had me walk up and then down a few stairs. On day four we walked even further and did more stairs and I decided I was ready for home. I asked my son to come and get me the next day. I didn't tell him that I had not yet informed my doctor of my plans, but as the doc was the person who had to discharge me, I soon had to.

I was well medicated, but that night, through the night, I woke in huge pain so instead of pushing the buzzer and waking half the world, I slipped out of bed and shuffled my way along with all the tubes and stuff nicely arranged on the IV cart, out to the desk, which as usual was deserted. In a room behind the desk were all of the night nurses, stationed in front of computers, typing away and discussing all kinds of things, like last Sunday's hangover, whose sister made out in an elevator and that one of the RN's had worked three shifts in a row. I listened for a bit, but being in too much pain to just stand there and listen to the gossip, eventually I did the hu-hum thing. There was no problem and within a couple of minutes, one of them came into my room with a couple of - - -whatever, which would numb the pain within a minute and I would again be off in dreamless sleep. I woke in the morning to day five. Last day, I thought. I wonder where that liaison nurse got to, I hadn't heard a word and I needed to know about home care, oh well, last day, last chance.

This is a catheter - it is inserted into the
bladder here and drains into a urine bag here
. . .

In came a whole wack of new students, young faced, good looking and eager to help. I told the one who looked like the ring leader that if I were to go home today, they would have to take my catheter, drainage tube, IV etc. out. "Oh, I'm sorry," said the big guy, "I didn't realize you were going home today", shaking his head and checking his clipboard.

He busied himself by relieving me of tubes while explaining to the remainder of the group as he slowly went about what he was doing. "This is a catheter," he explained, "it is inserted into the bladder - here and drains the urine into a bag - here so that the nurses can measure the amount of urine being produced by the patient and record same."

I had to close my eyes, or I would have burst out laughing at the group of fresh faced students, mouths open, gaping at a sixty-five year old woman having her catheter removed. Anyway, as soon as they were gone, I was still chuckling as I got dressed.

Then, in came the surgeon on his rounds. "Now, what am I hearing about you going home today?"

"Yes, I am if you will sign me out, I will be out of your hair. Sorry, I shouldn't have said that. But don't worry most men are touchy about baldness."

"Well, I'll tell you what", he said without a smile, "you are right, your recovery has been excellent. Now if you can get out of bed alone, push your IV cart down the hall, go up six stairs, turn come back down, and walk back to your room I would say you are strong enough to go home."

The poor fella didn't realize that I had done that yesterday. Piece of cake. I got out of bed, felt around and put

If you will sign me out, I will be out of your hair!

on my sneakers as my slippers had gone out full of shit with the waste. I transferred the only tube remaining and pushed the cart out and down the hall. At the bottom of the stairs, I removed the bag of saline from the cart, slowly climbed the stairs with the bag in my left hand and hanging onto the rail with my right. At the top of the sixth stair, I had to have a chat with myself.

"Well, self, sometimes you are too damned bold and stubborn. Now, you are dizzy, so stand here and rest before you start back down. What the hell are you going to do if you fall down those stairs?" "Oh shut up," I answered myself, " I may be bold but, by God, I am strong like bull"!

I looked down to the bottom of the stairs and there a small group had gathered, at least three or four of them - well, that's a group. Hanging onto the rail for dear life, I started back down. Slowly, slowly, one step at a time, I made it. I thought the small group was there to cheer me on but actually they were waiting for me to get the hell out of the road so they could go up the stairs. The rest of the test, back to my room, I could have almost run. The saline bag re-hung, I pushed the cart back into my room, re-plugged and got back into bed. Yes, I am going home.

Still attached was my IV which is always left in until the very end just in case any drugs need to be administered directly. I think they leave it in just so that you can't escape. Imagine walking down the street trying to hide the damn thing inside your jacket. No, I don't think so.

I realized that I was pretty weak when it damn near killed me to pick up my suitcase from the locker and put it on the bed. Looking into the mirror, for the first time, I

I strong, like bull . . .

could see the incision, all red and swollen and sore like hell. It went all the way down my back to just about even with lower part of my left breast (not counting the sag, which isn't too bad and I try hard to deny.)

I could sure use a shower. I hadn't had one since I left home. Obviously, there was no shower in my little bathroom and no one was offering to take me for one or help me, so I guess I don't need a shower. I couldn't possibly put my bra on as I never have been into self-inflicted pain, therefore, I got into undies, a pair of jeans and a loose T shirt. I decided to lay back on the bed and have a wee nap while waiting to go home. An hour later (or maybe two) in came the nurse with the clip board and happy face. "So, you are going home my dear, I need you to sign here and here and here". I signed - whatever - and dozed back off to sleep.

Steve arrived mid- afternoon and we went out to the desk. I felt pretty wonkey on my feet, but managed to fake it. The nurse said "take care" gave me a prescription for pain-killers and away we went down the elevator to the main floor drug store. I sat down before I fell down and Steve went and filled the script. We went up a level in the elevator where I told him that of course I could walk out. Oh my God, I was at the door swaying for fear I would fall down but followed him out to a small above ground parking lot and to his truck. There was no way I could climb in. He had brought along a pillow and quilt and lifted me up into the cab. I covered up and prepared for the four hour trip home. No problems, all good. I kept my eyes glued to the road and every time I thought we might hit a pothole, I braced myself by pushing my fists into the seat which

41

helped a bit, but five days in bed had reduced my muscles to pretty well nil and pot holes at the end of February, are unavoidable. With every one, I sang out "oh, God - bless you"! As each echoed pain throughout my body.

CHAPTER THREE

This is my Island, my home,
my light, my shore,
but tides that bring hope
and dreams that I adore
will now be lost for evermore.

Once home, Steve steadied me up into the house and I
lay on the couch with lots of pillows and a big friendly quilt
and fell asleep - ah, home sweet home. My two little dogs and
a huge black and white cat had been well taken care of by
my grandson, Zack and they seemed so glad to see me. They
jumped up with me and snuggled in. I have always thought it
awesome that animals have a way of knowing if someone is in
pain or where the hurting parts are. There we were, all four of
us on a couch, each in its own comfort zone and none bothering
the other except for the cat, Ziggy, who was so happy to see
me that he wouldn't stop purring and talking away with his
mam - mam merow. (Bet I never told you that my cat can talk,
limited vocabulary but very chatty.) There had to be one to piss
me off! He went on and on and after a while I told him to get
off the couch and leave me alone. He refused to go or shut up
so I gave him a little push in the right direction and reluctantly,
feeling rejected, away he went. Ah, silence, heaven.

Ziggy brought me a gift, some supper, fresh
and on the hoof!

Down in the laundry room, I had put a cat door in the window, so Ziggy could get in and out whenever he wanted. I mean, how do you argue with a cat? He will do whatever he wants anyway, or he will bug you forever to get his way.

I went to sleep and sometime later, I don't know how long, but I awoke to the purr, purr, mam, mam, merow again. I opened my eyes and there standing on the coffee table right in front of my face was Ziggy Puss with a live mouse hanging out of his mouth.

The poor mouse was wiggling and squeeking and struggling for his life.

I guess Ziggy wanted to get me a welcome home gift, so he brought some supper, fresh and on the hoof. Oh God, it hurt to sit up, it hurt to move, let alone laugh. I didn't want Ziggy to come on to the couch with the damned thing, it might get down between the cushions and oh God I didn't want to think about it. By now both little dogs were up and barking at it. JUST BLOODY WONDERFUL! I slowly pulled myself up and as I did, Ziggy dropped the mouse and it scurried off. Ziggy obviously wanted lots of love and praise and thanks for his gift. I totally ignored him, got up and went looking for the critter. After at least two whole minutes, I ran out of hunting strength and had to lie down again.

I said to myself; " Well girl, that little critter cannot be so foolish that he would dare go up onto the couch with two dogs and a cat up here, so lie back down and go to sleep". Lying back down, I noticed that two out of three of my bed mates were again asleep. Ziggy was back on the coffee table playing hockey with my glasses. He stick handled very well, passing from left paw to right and as he wound up to shoot, I grabbed him and plunked him down at the bottom of the couch so he could keep my feet warm. We all slept the rest of the night without any more excitement.

I figured with a nurse in three times a week to check my vitals, incision and help me shower, I would be fine at home. At home, I didn't have to run by anyone else's clock and could rest and eat and sleep whenever I needed. I had the phone right beside me and I did the best I could. Days passed and no-one came or called, so I looked up the number that I had been given for home care. As it was ringing on the other end, I was thinking "if my incision had become infected, I would have been dead by now!" The lady who answered the phone sounded puzzled. She took all my info including dates of the surgery, names of liaison nurse, doctors etc. and told me that she would have to call me back. Later that afternoon, the home care lady called to say that she was very sorry, but I had never gone back on the list. Had my surgery, or surgeon been changed since I first contacted the office? Yes, the first surgery was to be laprosocpic, but the size and position of the tumor, he couldn't do the operation. I had to have a full surgery. I told her that the nurse did not show up at QE2 in Halifax, before or after I had my operation. She told me she was sorry, but QE2 had not informed them of my changed surgery and it would take a while to process my request. In the meantime, I should go very quickly up to Emerg if I am coughing up blood, see any oozing, blood or puss coming from my incision, (like, it's on my back lady, kind of hard to see), if I were running a temperature, short of breath or passing out.

"Well, O. K. then, I'll do that!" I laughed and told her "Never mind, thank you I will take care of myself, I maybe two bricks short, but I strong like bull!"

Steve dropped in one morning and asked if I had emptied my garbage, "because something stinks rotten in here." I hadn't noticed, but he took the containers outside, emptied them, and sprayed them with bleach. There now, that should do it. But it didn't. A couple of days later, I could smell something rotten in my kitchen. I checked for a bad apple in the bowl, rotten potato in the bin, what the hell could it be.

On his next visit, Steve told me that it smelled like a dead animal and if we didn't find it, one of the dogs or the cat could get disease or poisoned. It suddenly hit my fog filled brain - the mouse. The mouse that Ziggy brought in as dinner for me that day I came home, remember, oh yeh?

We did a sniff and search and by deduction, Steve figured it had to be under the fridge. He pulled the fridge out and there was the poor little rotten critter. He was so decomposed that he flushed on the first try and yes, I gave him some last words, not nice words, but words 'magine.

My brothers and sisters called me quite often and just to hear their voices gave me a boost. My sister, Jean called and asked me how I was feeling. "Well, Jean, I am pretty good, but if I sneeze, it really hurts like hell where they took the ribs out."

"Well," she answered, "When I sneeze, I piss my pants, which would you prefer"? Point made.

I could no longer live without income. On week three after surgery, I brought one of my "people" home. She was a sweet little lady in her seventies, Annie. Lovely smile, and, being human, she could get a bit demanding every once in a while. I didn't have any problems adjusting to work again. I was up at six thirty to get used to it and could always take a nap in the daytime when she was at her day program.

I was gaining strength and feeling better as each day passed, so I brought home another lady. She had been suffering from schizophrenia since childhood. She also had a lot of physical limitations as she had cerebral palsy and although her movements were at times limited, well into her forty's she was very strong and could walk for miles. She was stubborn and within the limitations of her own mind, knew all there was to know about everything.

Next home was a sweet man in his mid-forty's, however, he required a great deal of care along with huge amounts of acceptance, help and patience. He would pee anywhere and everywhere, had to be bathed every morning and every few weeks, he would seizure for dangerous lengths of time, sometimes up to five minutes.

On this morning as usual, I woke him for his morning bathroom routine and then breakfast. He was always first up as he had the most serious problems and therefore took the most time to care for and the longest to shower. He came down the hall, into the bathroom and went into a seizure. If this wasn't yet a crisis situation, it was about to become one. Along came one of the gals who was obviously mentally distressed. The result was I had a major nose bleed and one of my bottom teeth went through my upper lip. How do you blame a mentally ill woman who you had taken willingly into your home and had provided care to for over a year? I was just plain not strong enough.

I instructed the Para-medics to take Emily to the hospital and have her admitted to the Mental Health Unit. I would go up as soon as possible.

It took a few minutes to explain to police that I couldn't go to Emerg to be checked out as I still had two mentally disabled people in the house to care for, to get up and going to their day programs. They got the picture when a hungry fella walked into the living room totally naked with a full colostomy bag.

My day went on, I cleaned up the male exhibitionist and got the princess up and dressed, administered meds, did charts, shaved the mister and brushed the missy's hair, fed them scrambled eggs and got them ready for the mini bus to pick them up for day care. I called my supervisor and told her what had happened, then drove up to Emerg. to make sure the admission went O.K..

While I was there, they checked my incision and put a stitch in my lip which although not bleeding was a wide gap. It was black and blue for a bit.

The scar is still there, so unknown to others, I bless that gal every time I look in the mirror or put on some lipstick which is seldom as both scare me.

I told my supervisor that I could not ever have her back in my home and that I would have to think very hard about if I was able to take proper care of the others. I did think on it and I thought for a long time. With no income,

I would have to sell my home at the shore. I would have to settle for a senior's apartment or a trailer and cut down all expenses.

My male stripper became quite ill and by March had been admitted into long term care and I decided to keep my princess Annie with me so that I had a bit of income and we could keep each other company. Over the years I had become quite attached to Annie, she had been such a dear sweet soul.

I stood at the window and watched the two men putting up a "For Sale" sign on the front lawn and tears welled up. What could I do? I spoke out loud with anger "this rotten disease has taken away my dreams, my home, my little corner of the world, the place I love. This is my shore, my road, my lighthouse, mine".

O. K., enough anger. I walked carefully down the bank to the shore and sat on my rock. The place I go to meditate, to be alone with God, to thank him for all the wonders of the sea and the blessings in my life. Oh, Jesus, girl, would you shut up before you drive yourself crazy! It is a cold grey day and I thought about my old uncle yelling at me "Susie, don't sit on them cold rocks, you will get bleeding piles so you will."

So I have to admit I am sick. I can't take care of the big five-bedroom house and I can't work to bring in the dollars so I can't pay the mortgage. Therefore the house has to be sold. So, once the house is sold, I will find a small cheap trailer (unless the kids talk me into a seniors apartment) and even if I say yes, I'll be lying and somehow work out my own plan, if the good Lord is willing to give

Susie, don't sit on them cold rocks, you'll get bleeding piles so you will!

me the time. I thought about cancer and prayed for all those suffering and dying room it. The wind picked up and I shivered, suddenly needing to pee. I had to climb up the bank on all fours although it was painful, I was laughing and going as quickly as I could toward the house. No, no, you can't pee your pants - for God's sake, you haven't peed our pants since you were four years old. No - no just squeeze that thing together, grab it, tell it to hold on, you can't let go. Quick, quick, into the house, down the hall, oh God, oh God, it's coming - into the bathroom, pulling, yanking at the pants. I sink to the floor and feel the hot flow of urine soaking my jeans and forming a large pale yellow puddle on the white tiled floor. I started crying. I yelled "Mom, I need you Mom, you are not here and I need you right now, I need to talk to you about something important, because I have cancer and it is about to take my house away!"

I knew that it would break my heart to sell the house. It was the most beautiful spot in the world with the ocean only a hundred feet away. I loved watching the constantly changing tides and views from every room including sunrises, sunsets, amazing cloud formations and storms coming in. That shore was heaven to me. Whenever I could, I went down and sat on the huge rock, meditating, praying, dreaming, just drinking in the silent beauty. But, I knew I had to sell it. With cancer, I could no longer work and therefore, couldn't make the payments.

The sign went up and I spent most of the summer having yard sales, giving stuff away, and making runs up to the Salvation Army Thrift Store, and the Re-store. It was hurting my heart to do all this, so I tried to keep my emotions in neutral. Don't think, don't feel and just keep going, one foot ahead of the other, keep going. I tried to stay focused on my purpose in life which was simply to live.

The house sold that fall and after all was said and done, there was just enough money to buy a cheap old trailer, and I mean cheap and old. My budget had to be shaved very close to praying at the end of the month. The new owners would not be taking possession of the house until the end of March, which would cost me rent, imagine renting your own house, but that's the way life is. Packing small boxes so that I could lift them myself went pretty slowly. I knew that I was not working hard at it, after all, I had no energy, my heart wasn't in it. I started moving small stuff to the trailer in my car. How do I take the peace, joy and dreams that I felt in the house at the shore, and fit them into at forty year old fourteen-foot-wide-trailer? I just didn't know how, so once again I just kept going and going. Think only of the positive, no negative stuff allowed in my head. I had to make this my home and make the best of it.

Some nights, every muscle in by body was aching. Even muscles that I didn't have. During my surgery, some of the nerve bundles had been severed and the nerve pain was huge. My doctor prescribed pain management medication (not the heavy duty pain-killers, not that kind, the kind that I had to take on a constant basis), although the pain would get so bad I would have taken anything - well almost.

During that spring, while the ground was still frozen, a construction company had begun work along the shore, bringing in huge loads of rock and banking up the mega fancy homes along the shore to the east. As our shore was the best and safest way for people to walk down to the beach, and also to take smelt shacks and machinery down, they did, and they wrecked it. I had planted bulbs and mint at one end and my three little nephews and their dad had built steps and placed rocks in the right places which made it much easier to walk down, however the bank was filled with machine tracks and clay now, steep and slippery.

After the machines moved out, I would walk down to the bank above the shore and just stand there wishing I had the strength to get down there and back up. My time in my house was running out. It was time to talk to myself again. "Self, I said out loud, you are whining. All you do is complain about this. Come on, woman, if you want to go down, then get your ass down there". This was my favorite place in the whole world and cancer had taken away my home, this would always be my shore and I had to have the strength to be there.

I went over to the right a few feet to where there was some fairly long grass (as if holding on to it would take my weight), anyway, I took a couple of steps toward the bank and as if in slow motion, I lost my balance and started slipping on the grass and clay, on my bum. I got the slide under control by digging my heels into the dirt and shuffling my ass down to meet them. Who said I have a well-padded ass, well - - maybe. Little by little I reached the shore. I knew that if I fell, I would be in big trouble, but I didn't and I wasn't.

I sat there on my rock for a long time. Sometimes thinking about cancer, sometimes about death. I thought that life is like a short story, it just gets interesting and it is over. The trick, I guess is to be happy day by day with the story of your own life. This is it, right? You are born, you live and you die. No matter how many years, or months or days in between, that is the way of nature, of God.

The tide was coming in so I started back up the bank, trying this time to watch my footing so I wouldn't fall. I had to laugh thinking of the next day's Wayne Wright cartoon in the next morning's news Journal Pioneer: "A sixty six year old Summerside woman had to crawl up the bank from the shore yesterday. She didn't appear to be injured, however onlookers noted that although there was no man in sight at the time, that the seat of her jeans was covered in grass stains."

Ha, ha, I could be so lucky.

I didn't have to move until the end of March and so, Annie and I moved slowly into the trailer. I still had a lot of work to do, but I didn't have the energy of a wet noodle, and procrastinated over and over again. By the fall, I had a lot of headaches in the temple on both sides. They would sometimes last for days. The old pain in my ribs was back and I was thinking that I really didn't feel well and went to see Doctor Kelly. He booked me for a "routine x-ray" and a few weeks later for a "routine CT scan" of both my chest and brain. About a week after the scan, he called me to say the head scan was o.k., there were some markings that we would explore later, but there was something on the chest picture. Not something to panic about, just something. He told me that a surgeon would be calling me in the next little while to book an appointment for a "just in case" biopsy.

. . . there were no men in sight
at the time, but the seat of her
jeans was covered in grass stains.

I hate that word, biopsy. Say it slowly, bi-opsy. It sounds like a two-sided oopsy. Anyway, it is a word that puts fear into the heart of millions every year. Weeks passed - no word. I started praying that it was nothing and no-one had bothered to call about nothing.

I also absolutely hate waiting. If you know one way or the other, then you can prepare yourself for the outcome. But not knowing is pure torture. I called my doctor's assistant and asked. She said she would have him call me. He did and told me that he had tried to find a surgeon to perform the biopsy, but no-one would touch it. Then he tried to find an oncologist who also declined the case. He got in touch with the surgeon in Halifax who answered that the re-occurrence of cancer in my left lung was inoperable as it was very close to and perhaps attached to the aorta (the main artery to the heart.)

I have two little dogs, both chihuahuas, Zara and Maggie, along with the beast of a cat, Ziggy Puss. All three of them are very precious to me and they bring me huge amounts of love and comfort. When a person has a serious illness, having pets can mean a great deal, not only in giving the person a feeling of closeness and companionship, but also giving the person reasons to be there, to care for them and know that they are dependent that person just to be there. I love all three of them very much. Just seeing them all together, curled up and sleeping warms my heart.

One November afternoon, and I was reading the paper at the kitchen table when I heard Zara, choking. I hurried into my bedroom where she was on my bed and couldn't seem to get her breath. She was close to panic. I checked her mouth, nothing, wrapped her in a towel and drove as fast as I dare to the animal hospital, with her laying there in my lap. She only lived for a few minutes after we arrived. Her heart had given out. I was thinking - - - no, no, Zara, it is me who is ill, not you this should not be your time to die.

I felt a huge sadness as I paid for the cremation and drove home with tears streaming down my face feeling that a little piece of my heart was missing. It still is.

CHAPTER FOUR

Walk on through the wind, walk on through the rain
tho your dreams be tossed and blown
walk on walk on with hope in your heart
and you'll never walk alone.
Rodgers & Hammerstein

On December 10, I met with the Radiation Oncologist from the Cancer Center in Charlottetown who very patiently answered all of my questions. He showed me the pictures of my lungs and tumor and showed me from different angles how dangerous it would be to go in surgically. It was inoperable, therefore we had only one option, which was to treat it with aggressive radiation and chemo. Firstly, they would be done at the same time to complement each other so this would be done in Charlottetown for about seven or eight weeks, every day, with a rest on weekends. Over that time the oncologists would keep assessing my progress. This radiation oncologyst has to be one of the kindest men on earth. He answered every little question, no matter how trivial, and treated me with so much kindness and respect that it touched my emotions. He told me that I would have to go back to Halifax for another PET scan. After that, I would be getting a call from Charlottetown Cancer Treatment

Center and they would set up my calendar and appointments. I would be going through a regime of intensive radiation along with chemo at the hospital in Charlottetown. This meant going down every morning for at least six weeks. I would be getting generally one, sometimes two sometimes three treatments a day, after which my cancer would be reassessed, and then I would likely need more chemmo for about twelve weeks in Summerside.

Around the 15th of December, Annie told me that she would like to have our family picture taken for Christmas. Our family, meaning Annie, myself and Maggie. Two of the stores still offering photos ready for Christmas told me I couldn't bring a dog into the store. I convinced one gal that my little dog is a Therapy Dog and that I could bring along her registration. That was good enough and away we went. On the 22nd of December, we picked up beautiful shots of the three of us. Maggie, our little Chihuahua posed as if she were a pro and Annie looked happy and healthy.

Annie expressed to her workers at her Senior's day program that she was afraid I would die and there would be no-one to take care of her, and that if I died, her worst fear would be that she would have to go into the Manor. We talked about it and I took both her hands in mine and told her that I was not going to die, that it was not at all part of my short- term plan. Well, maybe someday, because everyone dies at some time, but I had a lot of good years yet to go.

Over Christmas we had fun with Steve, Janice and the grand-children, with lots of laughs food and wine and no-one even spoke the C word. A couple of days after

Christmas, Annie became ill. She was running a temperature and had a deep painful cough. The next morning I drove her up to emergency at PCH. I took her by wheelchair into the triage nurse who took all of her info and warned us that this illness was very serious, apparently they had diagnosed a super bug that would not respond to antibiotics and it would be a long time before a doctor could see her. The waiting room was full, totally packed and it seemed that all of the people were wearing a mask and echoing Annie's horrible deep cough. A man at the end of one of the rows gave up his chair for me, for which I was very thankful as I could sit and keep the wheelchair right beside me.

We waited and waited. I went back and forth to the washroom and wet a paper towel to wipe poor Annie's forehead. She was sweating hugely, but didn't want her coat off. She was refusing even a tiny drink of water and just wanted to go home and go to bed. After about five hours, Annie started crying and asking me over and over to please take her home to bed. How does a person tell a seventy four year old mentally disabled woman that it was best to stay at the Hospital and wait? She continued to cry.

I spoke to the triage nurse who told me it would be another five or six hours before she would see a doctor, and if I was willing to take her home, give her lots and lots of water, Tylenol and her regular meds, then call her family doctor first thing in the morning making sure I gave him all the details.

I got up during the night. She was sleeping and not coughing as much which was a good sign, but it was time for her Tylenol. I took in her pills and a drink of water with a straw. She didn't wake all the way up, but took the pills and said "I hope I didn't give it to you! I don't want to make you sick, I need you to be here with me."

"No, no of course not." I kissed her forehead goodnight and tucked her in.

At six -thirty, I called an ambulance. She was refusing even tiny sips of water. Her bladder was failing and there is a certain smell to urine after the kidneys have shut down. I didn't have a great deal of strength but somehow lifted her into the wheel- chair in time for the ambulance. In the trailer the Medics would not have been able to get the patient bed down the narrow hall. I moved my car out of the driveway and pushed her in the chair out to the door as the EMS pulled up in front. They kept taking her vitals, BP, heart rate, respirations and recording same, while I just held her hand and talked to her. "You will be just fine, darlin, just wait, you will be back at home right soon." She asked for our little dog, Maggie, who I picked up and placed on Annie's lap. She kissed her and held her to her face. The paramedics handed the dog to me and brought in a chair so that they could carry Annie down the back steps. I told them I was right behind them.

At the hospital, they had Annie in Critical Care where they were doing what they needed to do. I answered as many questions as possible and sat with her not knowing what to say. I went out to the lobby and called her brother who was her next of kin.

After I had been up almost twenty four hours, I started nodding off in the chair and felt very relieved that Annie's sister-in-law had come to relieve me, I went home and right to bed. The nurse was to call me if her condition changed.

Throughout the time that poor Annie was dying, she remained in the emergency department as there were no available beds in the hospital. When a hospital is responding to a super bug, all infected patients must be kept in areas that will not affect the remainder of the hospital.

I went in next morning, sat and held her hand and kept talking to her. I brushed her hair, put some lipstick on her, kissed her forehead and told her she looked like a million bucks, she smiled. The nurse came in and we rolled her over to her other side for her comfort. I washed her face and hands and feet and she squeezed my hand. Her niece came in and sat with me and an hour or so later, blood seeped from the corner of Annie's mouth which I wiped clean with a wet face cloth. I also cleaned off her teeth, poured tiny drops of water into her dry mouth, kissed her forehead and she dozed off to sleep. The nurse whispered to me "it won't be long now".

For seven years, Annie had clung to me for her every need and I had always been there for her. Now, she clung to my hand as if drawing strength from me. I had joked with her a lot over the years, about living and dying and becoming an angel, but now, I had to be serious. I whispered: "Annie, you have to listen to me dear, I know how you love me, and little Maggie, and we both want you to come home to us, but when God comes and takes your hand leading you to heaven to be and angel, I want you to smile and go with Him knowing that I will always love you. When God calls me home, I know you will be there to meet me. Just think of it, a long flowing white dress and wings. You already have your hair brushed and lipstick, you already look like a beautiful angel, so you are ready, O.K. little darlin'?"

Annie's breaths became more and more shallow and within about five minutes, she let go of my hand. That was December 30, 2013 and when I got home there was a message on my machine that an appointment had been set up in the PET scan department of QE2 in Halifax for a scan. All I could think of is that we had to bury Annie first. Please dear God give me strength and could you please stop testing me for just a little bit until I catch my breath? I cried my heart out.

After the funeral, I didn't cry. Annie had her wish and I kept my promise. I had not died and left her and she didn't have to go into the manor. The Lord moves in mysterious ways!

As I was now an old pro at going to Halifax and not a bit scared, I decided to take the shuttle van over. It worked out perfectly, and Steve didn't have to take a day off work. I met the van at Read's Corner at 7 a.m. got to my appointment at 1 p.m.. Back on the van at 3:20 and back home at 7:20 p.m. Yippee, this is so much fun.

The next appointment was for a week later in Charlottetown. I went in for radiation mapping, tattoos, and to see the Chemo oncologist. Janice, my daughter in law drove me down and stayed with me. She is always in good spirits and up for a laugh. The first part, in radiology went O.K., they made computer maps of my non-existent upper lung, scar tissue and whatever was left on that side, paying particular attention to the new tumour. They tattooed locations on my boob which of course, I was wanting to brag to my grandkids about, having a tattoo - and on my boob - wow! No, not the ugly one, the other side.

Anyway, then they made a mold of my upper body and head from a blue plastic bag with pliable foam inside. They explained that this would be a pillow that would fit my head and shoulders and with my hands above my head, I would not move during my radiation therapy.

Next, we sat and answered questions with regard to stress. I tried to explain that I had just been through a difficult death and all of my stress was not due to cancer.

A nurse called my name and took us into a waiting room to meet with the doctor. Next - Oops!, it felt like several hours later, in he came. I couldn't blame him, he had traveled in from across and he was not a young man. He asked questions and then said "you have lesions showing on your brain. So, you have been having mini-strokes." I looked at Janice and she at me and I said "not that anyone has told me, no, no mini-strokes."

"Well, I am telling you, you have been having mini strokes. Are you taking low dose Aspirin every day? - - yes? well, that is because you are taking mini-strokes."

Janice turned to me so he could not see. Her eyes got "that look" which means what kind of new story is this? I had to bite the inside of my cheeks not to laugh.

"Anyway", he went on, "jump up on the exam table I need to listen to your breathing". I sat on the edge of the table and as I moved my feet up, a huge rumbling loud fart escaped. Didn't mean to, it didn't even sneak out, only God

. . . they tattooed locations on my boob, no, not the ugly one, the other side and made a mold of my upper body . . .

decides on the release of mega farts like that one - it came with a force. You know what I mean? Well sir, that was enough for Janice, she couldn't hold back and, as the doctor walked out through the door, we both burst out laughing. "You have to stop laughing, or you will shit your pants and have a mini-stroke. Sue, do you hear what I am telling you, a mini-stroke." We both laughed until we cried. The "mini-stroke" thing lasted all the way home to Summerside and one thing about a good belly laugh along with tears is it is good for your soul and takes your mind off the C-word. It also relieves huge amounts of stress and by the time we got home, I could feel the calm and when I went to bed that night, I knew that I was ready to go on with the fight.

Only God decides on the release of mega farts
like that one, it came out with a force!

CHAPTER FIVE

KEEP WALKING

Keep putting one foot ahead of the other,
go on from day to day.
Keep saying "I can do this
no, there is no other way".
Don't ever think of quitting
keep saying in your mind
"God help me, I can do this,
I can leave this hell behind -
and keep on walking.

The chemmo room at the Charlottetown Cancer Centre is quite comfy, with big recliners and a pillow on every chair. First the nurse wraps your chosen arm in a hot towel to make a vein pop and then inserts an I.V. and hangs a bag of saline. A few minutes later, she comes back and hangs a bag of pre meds. When the machine beeps that the pre meds are finished, the line is flushed with saline and she hangs another bag, containing the chemmo drugs. Volunteers kept coming around and offering a warm blanket, tea, coffee, anything from the kitchen. A volunteer around my age, a very good looking man asked me if I would like anything so I asked him if the bar was open. He laughed and said, "not yet". "When it does," I replied, "could you please bring me a Blue?" After my chemmo treatment, I was heading down the hall toward radiation when the same good- looking volunteer came up behind me. "Sue, Sue, just the lady I have been looking for".

"Will you still feel that way in the morning"? I asked, "or are you bringing the book I left in chemo"? I thought it quite funny, he was obviously very married but he did laugh, and such a handsome laugh!

It is one hundred and fifty five steps from the front desk at the Cancer Treatment Centre in Charlottetown to the radiation waiting room. There are two radiation areas, one Blue, the second Yellow. I was on the yellow list, yellow file and yellow waiting room.

On this day in the yellow waiting room there was a full house. One gal was sitting on the end table. We were all talking about cancer and what it has meant to our lives and to our children. A few tears and heartfelt empathy flowed around the room along with a whole lot of warmth and hugs.

There was a lull in the conversation and I said

"Sh sh can you hear it? I can hear it, can you? If you listen, you can hear it and sense it and feel the love in this room, the love between us all as we share the sadness, nightmares and fear along with cruel unknown outcomes of this disease".

On this particular, Wednesday, week two, treatment number six, I walked down the hall behind a young couple, possibly in their mid twenties. Oh my God, that young and going through all this pain and suffering! I prayed that they

Just the lady I have been looking for!

were here to visit someone not for treatment, or God help them. I couldn't help notice her cute little bum swinging up left and up right as she walked in her second skin lycra blue jeans and high heeled boots. I was trying to figure out how she did it, so me being me, I had to try it. Walking behind, with no-one behind me to see, I practiced the 'squeeze the cheeks together, lift right cheek as right foot steps ahead, then lift left cheek as left foot steps ahead, then start over.'

One more and one more and a nurse tapped me on the shoulder. "Whoa, you got it girl, work that tush" - - Ooops busted.

Today I feel sad and alone like a needy child. I should feel happy today as this is my fourth and final week of chemo in this round of treatment, now I just had to finish my weeks of radiation. For some reason,

I got all melancholy in the treatment room. I was the only one sitting there alone. Everyone else had a husband, girlfriend, daughter, parent, except me and to tell the truth, I was envious, a little jealous even. They sat with their sick loved one and brought them a warm blanket, or a cup of tea and a cookie. My kids live in Summerside, both have full time demanding jobs and three teenaged kids home to drive them around the bend. Still, I sat there and the other patients held hands, patted shoulders and rubbed feet - could it possibly be that this old bird is jealous. They all have someone and I have no-one and it is not fair. I was on the verge of tears, but talked myself out of making that ugly face it would have made them all either laugh or cry. It is the same ugly that puts the fear into dogs and small children. For God sake girl, suck it up!

Squeeze the cheeks together as left foot steps ahead,
lift left cheek and repeat for right side.

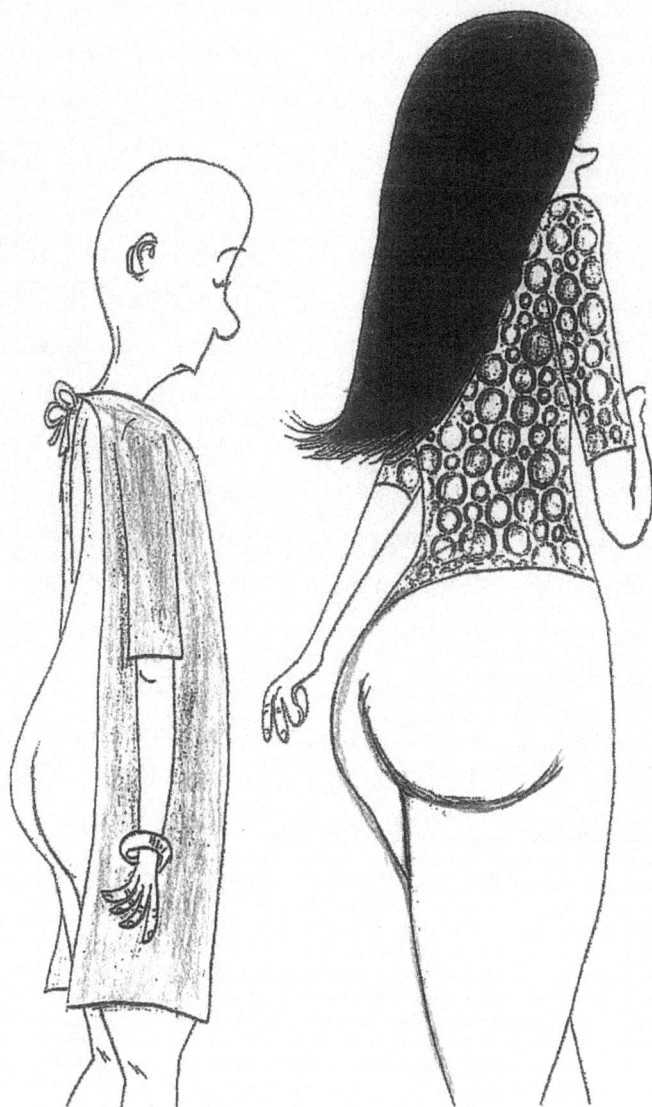

My chemo takes about two hours. From there I go directly to radiation, put on a johnny shirt and wait to go into the yellow radiation waiting room. In the waiting area was a lady with her daughter and my aloneness just worsened. The daughter, about twenty or so, gently took her Mom's coat off and hung it up. She took her Mom into the booth and helped her change into her j-shirt, after which they came out and sat down, waiting hand in hand, such a touching scene, I had to leave. O.K., if my legs would grow longer, I would kick my own ass, but that won't happen any time soon.

In the washroom, I let the flood of tears go. Tears for the other patient and tears for me. Why, God? Why does everyone have someone here who cares except me? I looked in the mirror and told my self - because you are ugly for Christ sake, you have no hair and you are old; you have a huge ugly scar all the way down your back and your right tit is weird and looks like a saggy bag of fat with a bite taken out of it. That brought a small smile from the old girl in the mirror and I blew my nose and went back to the waiting area. The drive home takes about an hour depending on traffic and weather conditions. For some reason, that afternoon seemed like forever. The kind man driving the car kept just under the speed limit "just in case" and I felt he needed to keep talking to me just to keep me company, all I wanted to do was sleep and let my mind go blank, no pain, no tears, just sleep, but out of respect for his kindness, I managed to keep a conversation going.

Each day, those who had to travel to Charlottetown alone for cancer treatment were driven there and by a volunteer from the Masonic Lodge. Each day, these men were willing to pick us up from our homes, help us into the vehicle and drive us to the door of the Cancer Center. They drove through snow and freezing rain and cheerfully delivered us home again. This is a service for which I will be eternally grateful, as without them, one of the kids would have to take six or eight weeks off work to drive me.

The men driving us to treatments took turns and we got to know them as well as you can know a person in one hour down and one hour back. There were three of us and the back seat was the first taken as a person could sleep of and on or just check out for a while. I was telling them a story about going to the mall and asking if I could join the "old farts club". Danny said "No, you don't drink enough or fart in public". (Little does he know). It got a couple of smiles, but everyone was feeling really burned out. The driver chuckled and began to tell me about other cancer patients that he had driven from Summerside. He said I had a great attitude and he felt bad about my cancer as there have been a lot of deaths from cancer and wasn't I scared? I told him, "Not me, I strong like bull", he said with a laugh, "well, - - - maybe full of bull, but that could be what keeps you going, and smiling.".

On the trips back and forth, we learned a bit about the drivers, their wives names and how their kids and sometimes grand-kids had faired out along the bumpy road of life. One fella, Joe was a real joker. On the way back from Town, I sat in the front with another gal about my age in the back. Undergoing treatments at her age seemed so cruel, but woa here, she is my age, always had a smile and quite often brought along cookies, and other treats. (That is more energy than I had!) That day, on the way home, we passed a fella hitchhiking and Joe said "Oh darn, Elsie, we should have picked him up for you, you could have kept him company back there."

"Hell no," said Elsie, "its been a good long time since I had a man, I would likely have killed him." Some of the rides back and forth were worth the good laugh.

That day, finally home, I made a scrambled egg for supper, had a quick bath and went to bed around eight o'clock, but I couldn't sleep. I got up and checked my pill pack to make sure I had taken them.

"Memory loss or chemmo brain" (while taking treatments) is real and at times can be embarrassing, at times just handy. If I meet up with someone and I wouldn't have for the life of me remembered his or her name ten years ago (even if I were paid,) now I can say "sorry, bud, chemmo brain". O.K., it is a little tiny white one, but isn't life about turning negatives into positives? Anyway, my memory does fail me, sometimes, it is part of being half way around the bend.

I went back to bed and tried to sleep. Of course, if you try, it won't happen. The longer I lay there thinking, the more hyper and mad at myself I became. I kept thinking about my sons and my grandchildren, my paintings and writing, all I have ever lived for and devoted my life to, and about how much time we have on this earth. What is time? How could there possibly be no time left? I thought about giving birth and all of the sweet raw emotion involved in giving birth to a child. The feeling of them drawing life from my breast. Holding them, watching them grow to fall and get back up, to make me sometimes proud and sometimes ashamed. For Steve to grow into a man, a good man, marry and have children of his own. To know that a part of me, my flesh and blood remains forever with him, his wife and their kids and that they are and will always be part of me. For Scott, it has been his life choice not to marry or have children but I love him deeply all the same. I have never interfered in the choices they made. I just prayed they would be happy.

The message I wanted to give them all at this time was "you are not why I am alive, but you are all I ever lived for!" Time ticked on as it always has and morning came early. As the clock read six-thirty, I was begging for just one more hour. Darn, I had to have a talk with myself again. I said "get your ass out of bed, put some coffee on, shower, brush your teeth, feed the animals, let them out for a pee. Cook your egg and try your best to eat it, then get your ass ready to start another day of treatments." I can, I will beat this damned disease.

The tears and feelings of self pity passed and I soon came back as my quick thinking idiot self. I had knew that the main requirements for surviving treatments is attitude. I need to have the attitude that sais "what is, is and what will be, will be." I can and will live each day and take each step with determination, not a determined grimace, but a determined smile!

Something new and different was going on between my legs, no silly, not that, I couldn't pee. Speaking of down there, there was no hair where just a couple of months ago once there was at least some. All of the hair on my bod was gone. I keep telling myself that everything is O.K., but as I look at it in the mirror, I have never seen it totally hairless before at least not since I was eleven. I felt I needed to pee, but it wouldn't come out. Remembering the tricks after childbirth, I would run the tap, blow bubbles through a straw, think of something else, no pee.

Once the urine pressure became urgent, I had to hold a plastic container between my legs, and standing up, let gravity do its thing. Straddled over the toilet, once it got started, I tried pulling out the cup - - not a good idea in fact, a big mistake, as once it got going it couldn't or it wouldn't stop. Wow, the sheer volume amazed me. Did I ever tell you the story about the friend of mine who could drink eight beer without a pee? No, huh? - - well, never mind.

I had six weeks, five days a week of radiation and then six days of double treatments and then a final two days, twice a day of cutback (reduced fields). I was so, so tired. Now, yippee! at least two weeks off. Everyone at the Charlottetown Cancer Centre had been so good, I can't tell you how kind and understanding they are, always smiling and dedicated to the needs of the patients, and so ready to answer every question and always remembering everyone's name. When I went in for my final day of radiation, I took in Thank You cards for each department. No, I didn't cry, I was so thankful that it was over for a while, even though I had burns on my chest and back, I knew they would heal and I still had to do chemo in Summerside. I smiled all the way home. Yea, I cracked a few jokes to keep the other girls up, but deep down it was for me.

I would run the tap, blow bubbles, think of something else - - - no pee.

Just before I got my buzz cut, I went looking for a ball cap to cover my soon to be bald head. I found a green plaid one at the dollar store that I kind of liked, so I went all out and bought it. The dollar store is my favourite place to shop. I can totally ditch ten dollars there and go home with a bag of goodies without wasting one ounce of guilt. Anyway, in the second week of chemmo, every morning there was hair all over my pillow. I talked to one of the nurses at the Centre and she said, "If it's going girl, you might as well go all the way now, but don't forget, it's not all bad, you don't have to shave your legs, the wiry one's growing out of that mole on your chin, and fuzz on your top lip will also be gone". O.K. then, I thought, thank you so bloody much for mentioning all that, I really appreciated it, and I am especially happy that you noticed the upper lip, thank God I have never had any in my nose! Have you checked your nose lately? But I didn't say it.

That weekend, I asked my daughter in law to come and do the honours. She came and buzzed off the remainder of my hair. I didn't feel at all bad about my loss of hair, it's only hair, it will grow but so will the tumour in my lung if I don't fight it with everything I've got.

Now, done with six weeks of chemo and radiation, thank God, I needed to regain some strength and health and look forward to another twelve weeks of chemo here in Summerside. The big bonus to that was I don't have to travel, the hospital is about five minutes away. I was feeling really quite good the general opinion was that the tumor was shrinking and with this new round of chemo, maybe we could keep it from becoming active again. If it does come back, I will cross that bridge when I get to it.

Thank you so bloody much for mentioning the mole on my chin and hairs on my upper lip!

Have you checked your nose lately?

My time off really felt good. I gained a bit of strength and weight back. My blood tests look good, my oxygen intake was good! I walked little Maggie a bit further every day and started my exercise program. Some days I just couldn't do it, but every little bit of exercise is really good for my heart and one good lung. I would smile and say "Keep going, girl."

As it ended up, I had a month off between chemmo/radiation and the start of the next round of chemmo. It felt so good, I can't tell you, having short spurts of energy and sleeping much better. My hair even started to grow.

My friends and neighbours invited me out and I felt that my life was back to normal for a while.

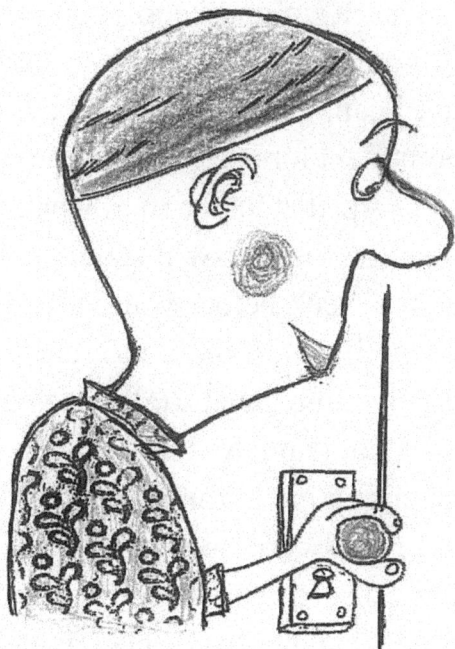

You are having a hair extensions party?

CHAPTER SIX

So, you suck it up and keep going and keep going until you think you can't, then you think of the little train and say "I think I can, I think I can, I know I can."

My appointment for cycle one chemo in Summerside was for the 17th of April at 9:00 a.m.. I waited in the comfy room and worked on the jigsaw puzzle, the same one as I had worked on the week before waiting to see the doctor. The lab lady came in and took blood samples and shortly after, one of the chemmo angels, (all oncology nurses have wings and halos), came out and took me on into the La-z-Boy room. She placed me in the corner and explained that if I was a good girl, I could come out of the corner next time. She asked a few questions about the other chemmo and the general stuff on her list. You could tell by her smile she was a bit cheeky and when the other girls would say, "here comes trouble", I knew she was my kind of people and I would get along great with her, not too many people are as crazy as I am.

My chemmo now takes six hours. I remember in Charlottetown thinking that two was long. Anyway, the nurse gets an IV going and then hangs a pre-med bag and gets it dripping. I close my eyes and listen to the beat - tic tic, tic tic, psht psht, over and over again. I try moving my feet to dance with tictic, tictic, psht, psht. Hey, I remember that beat, no problem. Then I looked around the room, praying that I didn't say that out loud. No-one was laughing - -saved again, thank you, God.

The timing was perfect. Janice works at the hospital and gets off at three. As you can't drive impaired, which you are considered after chemo, Janice stopped in to pick me up to go home. I didn't feel impaired or disabled in any way, but the ride home was good and I felt as if I had been at hard labour all day, so went to bed. I awoke around 8:00 a.m.

I lay there in bed for a couple of minutes thinking, O.K., I should feel rotten. I don't, what is going on. I got up, made coffee, brushed my teeth, put a slice of bread into the toaster and put the pan on to cook an egg. Still, I feel O.K, no headache, no morning sickness, not even nausea, nothing. Well sir, this is great. As the day went by, I felt a bit mentally off, sort of foggy, but other than that, (after all, I am a bit mentally off *without* chemmo) all was good.

I hadn't planned on going anywhere that day so I decided to take the mop and aggressively attack the dust bunnies that had been breeding in my house like the horny little prolific producers that they are. They are under all the beds, in the closets and places that I don't pretend to acknowledge. You never need to look for dust bunnies at my house, they grow so big that they jump up and bite your ankles. I saw a sign at a store uptown that reads: "Housework can't kill me, but I don't want to take any chances!" It is now on my fridge.

Taking a closer look at the specific make up, color and DNA of the bunnies, I realized that my cat and dog, respectively are black and blonde, both short haired. My hair, up until the middle of February was shoulder length, dirty blonde with gray taking over second place. So this new brood of bunnies was mostly due to the loss of my hair about three months ago. Boys oh boys I am good at growing bunnies, I should be selling them. Then, a most beautiful thing happened. Of course, a beautiful thing to me may be a crazy thing to you, so be for-warned. I took the dust mop out onto the deck and shook the hair out. A small gentle gust of wind blew little tumble-hair balls across the deck and they stuck to the top step. Just then, along came a tiny chickadee, no bigger than a minute and she gathered the hair in her beak and flew off quite proud of herself, no doubt. I was thrilled at the thought. Along with the horror stories of the destruction of our planet and loss of hair to chemmo, here God and Nature had worked together. The hair I lost to cancer would line the nest for brand new baby birds to begin their lives - - it filled my heart!

I didn't sleep at all well that night, my body was dead tired, but my brain would not slow down. To make it worse, Ziggy kept jumping up on the bed and kissing me with his worst ever mouse breath. I wanted to scream!

The next day was about the same except that I felt super hyper. I called the Cancer Centre and asked to speak to a nurse. I explained that I should be tired out, but I couldn't convince myself to get to sleep. The nurse told me that one of the drugs that I was taking made me hyper, and the side effect would only last for a couple more days. If I was still not sleeping then, to call back and they may have to give me another drug. On day three after chemo, I was so tired, I couldn't get my brain to focus on anything and barely keep my eyes open. I slept for about 18 hours, only getting up for meds, feed and water Ziggy and Maggie, not caring if they had bad farts or mouse breath. I would stagger to the bathroom for pee breaks, drinks of water or juice and back to bed.

My brave little dog Maggie, had to be O.K. with a puppy pad in the bathroom for a couple of days, but she is a sweetheart, other than the fact that she sleeps under the covers and farts a lot, she didn't mind. The numbness had started in my palms and on the bottom of my feet. It worsened slowly and became nerve pain in every muscle and joint in my body and then faded back into numbness. Actually, numbness was what I was hoping for, just sleep, blessed sleep. My brain was in a deep fog and I wondered about my santity. Thank God I'm good looking!

We will not discuss day four. I would slowly get better, I had to as week three after each round, I was due for another. My new - about three quarters an inch hair was coming out in hunks and chunks and I would look in the mirror and tell myself that I was a beautiful young woman with a great bod and even greater hair. I didn't believe it for a minute, and without eyebrows and lashes its hard to imagine, but I told myself anyway and prayed that God would forgive me for lying. If not, He would have to prepare Himself for a lot of "not too handsome people" who are clinging to a picture of "healthy and beautiful"!

So, you are telling me
you are strong like bull,
good looking, perfect
body except for one ugly
tit, could be pregnant,
super smart and a liar.

O.K. then!

So, I just laughed at myself and vowed to beat this C- devil. At least now, the ugly tit wasn't such a big deal.

Slowly, I got in touch with some of my radiation buddies. It had only been a few weeks. For one gal, the cancer had spread to her brain, or was hiding there all this time so her future didn't look good. I tried to cheer her up, but that wasn't easy. She wished me luck with my journey. Two of the radiation friends seemed to be in remission and very happy. I spoke to the daughter of the one lady from radiation who was sure she was going to die had finally been diagnosed with a benign tumor which had been removed. The tumour had been too close to her pancreas to be sure of a biopsy. The doctors had to reduce it with radiation so that they could get a better view and remove it.

My hair, or lack of it never did get me down, after all, it is only hair. However I went shopping with my granddaughter, Zabrina for a wig. We chose kind of light mousey brown with blonde highlights, after trying all different styles and colours and had lots of laughs. With the bright red one on, I just had to tell them that I could always go down to the warf and meet the Russian potato boats. I could make all kinds of money, but I would have to give a good big discount on account of the ugly tit and the mini strokes.

"I'll live to be a hundred, I told them all."

Cycle two - a little change to the premeds and I'm not in the corner any more so all must be good. The angels treated with care and love, and after six hours, I was done. At home I felt not too bad. Day one after, not great, but still nothing to write home about, not that anyone ever writes home anymore, or heaven forbid, writes back.

I could always go down to the warf and meet the Russian potato boats!

Here we go again, day two still not in pain or heaving. Day three, praying that the phone won't ring, day four - - oh my God. Memories of a mega hangover! Dizzy, dry heaves, pain from the dry heaves - - dehydration - - up to the hospital. Two bags of saline along with a healthy dose of anti nauseant and I was ready for bed for a good thirty hours. Still out of it, full of nerve pain and numbness, but promised Maggie I would walk her in the morning. O.K., I lied.

I am dragging my ass around making myself get through the day. Does the day run from first light to last light? That's not fair, I can't drag myself for that long. O.K., I think I will have to talk to God about this, I don't expect Him to just shorten the days for me. But why not? Don't I deserve it and he doesn't lengthen them in Saskatchewan. What do they have that PEI doesn't have. Oh, God, I hurt. I hurt so much. Every muscle in my body and every bone (including teeth I don't even have) is echoing nerve pain which hits especially at night. On and on and on, the next day and the next night. I don't know if I can keep doing this. At two in the morning I convince myself that I can't and then I remember that I have vowed to myself that I will keep fighting and keep fighting. So again, I talk to myself. I say "self, you beautiful woman with the gorgeous body and the brilliant mind you WILL WIN! And if you have any doubts, just ask yourself." (Just lets not mention the ugly boob. It upsets me to no end!)

On day ten, I felt somewhat better. I got up and didn't barf, that is major. I ate my poached egg and had two cups of coffee. Wow. As the day went along, I didn't feel normal, but I didn't feel ill. So, bonus. Hang in there.

Having a small yard at the trailer was new to me, so I went armed with my birthday money and picked up some flowers to plant and a nice, well shaped apricot tree. I have planted trees in memory of people in my life who pass away and I needed one for Annie. Most of them had to stay at the house at the shore, I haven't even gone down to see if they are still there. I have always turned away from and avoided heart break.

I bought some snap draggons, daisies, ivy to do up a couple of baskets, some parsley, mint and as a treat for Ziggy, a container of cat grass and another of catnip. I left the plants outside under the garden bench to get used to their surroundings.

Next morning I went out onto the deck to water my new little garden and there was Ziggy jumping up into the air and swatting at non existent things that apparently he thought he must catch. He was high as a kite. There was not one leaf left on the catnip plant, just stems sticking out of the dirt.

Don't tell me, after all I have gone through and put up with, now I have cat on drugs. He knows too that it hurts me to laugh.

So, on the 24th of May weekend, (it snowed on Saturday) Sunday was Mother's day and it wasn't warm, but it was sunny and I was ready to test myself with a spade.

First things first, I stepped in a large pile of dog shit. Maggie is a Chihuahua and if she goes outside or walked, her little poops are picked up after her. This rotten mush stuck to my shoes and made me start heaving.

In I went, pulled off the shoe with my other foot, down to the bathroom and threw up until my body ached. I really didn't feel like planting a tree today; I convinced myself that I didn't need my old garden shoes and gave myself permission to pitch them in the waste can.

I continued barfing until there was no more and then after dry heaves got me wobbling on my feet, I called Steve and Janice. Janice answered and I told her I needed help. I couldn't even walk straight. I was dizzy to say the least and had been dry heaving for hours. She told me to hang in there and Steve would take me up to Emergency. I am always worried about throwing up in someone's vehicle and even though nothing had come up for a while as there was nothing down there, I took a towel along with the plastic bag in my pocket. I could barely walk, so Steve pushed me in a wheelchair and the triage nurse took me into isolation as there was a flu bug person in the waiting room and I was doing active chemmo. (It seems that our hospital gets its share flu and super bugs.) All I wanted to do was sleep and as the nurse did my vitals etc. and hooked up an I.V. I kept dozing off. The doctor came in and had ordered a heavy duty anti nauseant. They hung another bag of saline and let me sleep. After a few hours, the doctor came in again and asked how I was feeling. I told him "much better," and "I am sorry I didn't do anything with my hair." He managed a grin and told Steve he could take me home. Steve left and went to the drug store for the six under the tongue instant melt anti nauseants which cost him over a twenty dollars for each pill. I had no time for Mother's day, it was cutting into my sleep, so once home, I got into bed and stayed there for almost twenty four hours. Finally on day eight, I felt a bit better. I ate my poached egg and kept in down, had small dishes of yogurt for snacks all day and by supper time, my belly was churning again. I put one of the wafers under my tongue and went to bed.

By day ten I felt much better but the nausea was still with me. The acid in my belly was really bad and I prayed that someday I would be normal. Of course I knew all my life that with me, there was no such thing as normal. I tried working out in the yard. After about twenty minutes, I would get weakness in my knees, elbows and wrists and I was just plain too weak to continue, so I would stand at the door and pray that one day soon, I could be out there at least kind of enjoying the sunshine. Don't get me wrong, I never have and never will give up hope, or faith, that I can and will beat this disease. Just sometimes it is hard to smile so I remind myself that I must smile anyway, God likes smiling people.

Feeling better after chemo is like a puppy humping a football, hang in there, be patient, this may take a while.

On day fourteen I went, armed with a bucket and spade, across the street to an empty lot and asked the neighbour, Merrick who was walking by with his dog if he would dig up May flowers and snow on the mountain and some other nameless plant for me that I could not let go wild over there. He dug them up and carried them home in a bucket to be planted in my front yard. Looking out now, they are quite happy here at their new home.

Day twenty, all my muscles that I thought I didn't have are aching. I look out into my yard in the rain and thank God that I could do that much. My neighbours don't know why I need to do these things on my own. They see me out in the yard or on the deck, or trying to cut grass (or shovel snow) when they have offered to help me. It is not so hard to understand. I had another long chat with God and I need to do as much as I can on my own. If I can't l will ask if I need help. Please, God let me do this for myself. I need to do things for myself. Chemo again tomorrow.

The doctor has given me a diagnosis of unconfirmed neurological damage to the nerve ending in different places in my body. It is called paraneoplastic. Apparently it is caused directly by the cancer. That rotten disease that has attacked my body is now sending out proteins or something that are attacking different nerves in my body. It is beyond me how the nerves on the sole of your feet can relate to a tumour in your chest cavity where your lung used to be or the scar tissue in your breast. But it does and it causes pain. I am a little concerned that the sight in my right eye has become blurry and sometimes I have floating blurs. When I have them, I don't drive for safety sake.

Nerve damage is something that I need to tackle after the cancer is beaten, or at least in remission. As long as the cancer is active it will continue to damage my nerves, if I can beat it, the damage will stop. Other than that fact, there is no cure or treatment. But, oh I am a determined bitch, I intend to beat it to death, death of the cancer I mean, not me, I still intend to live to be a hundred. Cycle three, day four. Armed with one of the wafer antinauseants thank you again to my son, I prepared for bed . To my way of thinking, my kids should not have to pay for my meds. This should not be happening to pensioners, or anyone else going through treatments. It makes me sad. I take along a bath towel (great for dry heaves) a yogurt container in case I have to pee in it several preparations to overcome the dry mouth, all been tried, none work, a couple of hunks of candied ginger to combat the acid, which does work, somewhat.

I was quite dizzy and just wanted to check out for today, at least. The cat and dog, (who I do remember have been fed), have snuggled in with me and we all manage to settle in with "good night John boy". The cat tries to tell me that his name is Ziggy, not John Boy but, even though I am fluent in cat, I am too damned tired to answer him.

The digital clock on my bedside table, the one with the large numbers for people who can't see a damned thing without their glasses, read 2:20 a.m., and the vomit flew all over my pillow and ran down the side of the bed. I could never have pulled this off in a single bed, but having no man, I have full command of a queen sized. So, not feeling very well at all, I have to admit to this, just don't tell anyone. I took my bath towel, covered up the puke as I couldn't stand the smell, (both the cat and dog had left the room for the same reason). Then, please promise you won't tell, but I knew that if I got out of bed, I would probably pass out. As I am fully aware that sixty eight year old cancer patients, when falling down, can quite easily break something, like a hip and die young. So I decided not to stand up, good choice. Now, if I died of complications from a broken hip, I would be extremely pissed off, because the main object of my life, right now, is to beat cancer. I lay there for a few minutes until the heaving stopped and I could read the clock again then I shuffled bum over to the other side of the bed. With my head now on a clean pillow, I pulled up the clean side of the quilt and slept until 6:30 a.m.. It didn't surprise me that neither Ziggy nor Maggie came back to bed. I woke up to that foul sour smell. Armed with another anti nausea wafer, I quicky stuffed my bed sheets and quilt into the washer, along with the towel. I pushed every button along with 'pre rinse' hoping that somehow any little chunks would somehow magically dissolve. If not plan 'B' was put them through another cycle. Also, I added an extra cap of the lavender fabric softener. I pulled a clean blanket from the closet and went back to bed. No sheets or pillow cases, who cares. At around eleven or so I realized that I had to get some liquids in my bod, plus I hadn't taken any of my morning meds. First I did small sips by straw of Gator drink which is supposed to replenish a person's hydration. I would sip away and then doze off for a few minutes follow with more sips. After about half of the bottle had stayed down, I celebrated by drinking some water and took my meds. There now, I knew I could do it. I even felt a bit stronger and put the load of laundry in the dryer, sweetly smelling of lavender.

Next morning around 5: a.m., the acid pain hit. Honest to God it feels like a person is taking a heart attack. When that person is me, it hurts like hell. The pain is at a nine out of ten and the only relief for me was to pound on my chest in the area of the pain hoping to move the acid and gas that had gathered there. I would try everything, many prayers, mainly consisting of "Oh God, oh God", double the liquid anti acid meds, eat antacids, chew on candied ginger, sip on ginger beer and do lots of heavy cursing. For some reason, the pain got a little less as I pounded - replacing pain with pain? I'm not sure, but if any of the doctors could see me now, they would say "totally insane for sure".

I walked around the trailer pounding my body until I suddenly felt I needed to power puke. Out it came, all over the bathroom floor, forced up by a huge, hard burp. Oh, thank you God, the release of gas had lessened the pain. I couldn't face cleaning it up right at that moment, so I reamed off paper towels, covered it up, turned the fan on and shut the door. Now I could lie back down and thankfully fall into a pain free sleep, it felt great.

Cycle three day seven. Not feeling pukie today, I just have a huge headache and limited sight especially in my right eye. No driving for me. My right leg gets nerve pain from my feet up into the ankles, then the knees, then all the muscles. I can handle it unless the calf muscles cramp. While I was preggers, I couldn't reach the muscles to massage them or anything, now I realize it wouldn't have done any good anyway. This has been the very worst of all the treatments. Is the word "worst" usable, somehow I remember my grade seven teacher telling me you can't use worse, worser, worsest. But anyway, at this point, who cares.

I went to bed just after 8:30 and a nice warm bath. Almost immediately, the pain hit my fingers and toes and moved up to the muscles and knees and elbows and shoulders and on and on. Nerve pain, oh God this is even worse than migraine. I took tylenol, pushed on my pressure points, cried and prayed, this pain was unbearable. I dozed off and on in pain all night, then got up about 7:30 and drove up to the hospital. Walking into oncology, tears were streaming down my face, I couldn't go on like this. I sat with the head angel (god love her) and told her I couldn't go on. She quietly wrote down every word I said. " It felt as if someone with plyers is pulling out my finger and toe nails. The bottoms of my feet are numb so I feel unsteady as if I am walking about a half inch above the ground. My hands are pretty well numb or tingling. The scars from my carpel tunnel surgery on both hands are giving big pain as well as the baby finger on my right hand that had been severed, degloved and re-attached some ten years ago is full of pain. "Just to pee brings on severe pain from my shoulders down my arms and into my hands. It lasts for about a minute and then goes away."

"I have been sporting false teeth for at least ten years and each and every one of those non existent teeth are aching all at the same time. The pain from my feet goes into my ankles and up into my knees and calves. It is horrible." I cried on and on. "I can't go on, I can't"!

She rubbed my back and told me that I needed to do this, I needed to vent. All the pain and puke had to come out and no one said cancer would be easy, but once I could explain all of my pain and get it out, I would calmly decide to go on with the fight. The angel left me to think about this for a few minutes and went to the computer and came back to tell me that it sounded like the same nerve damage that was caused by the cancer that I had been diagnosed with. My oncologist had been away for a break and a fill-in doctor was on duty to see all of us "in pain and unhappy" cancer patients. "O.K., I am going to give you a prescription for a supply of pain killers, also an anti anxiety pill that will help you sleep." I went away with mixed feelings, but in so much pain that I would have taken anything - almost.

A few weeks ago I had been diagnosed with a paraneoplastic disease which, as the doctor explained, develops when the cancer puts a protein into the blood stream that attacks the nerve endings in the body. This disease can save lives if there is nerve pain in areas of the body which cannot fit a diagnosis and if the patient is sent for a scan, it can show cancer and therefore the cancer can be treated immediately. However, it can produce very painful damage to the nerve endings in different parts of the body and therefor leaves the patient in extreme pain.

For my final dose of chemo for this round, the doctor cut out the one drug which is the most powerful and nasty drug in my list and I didn't react too badly except for the damned old nerve pain. I had minimal vomiting but the acid problem was still bad. It was now time to take care of the small stuff like a mouth full of thrush and cankers which I was treating with "swish and swallow" medication as the anti fungi drug which was to battle the fungus that had spread all the way down through my body.

This nerve disease is very painful and is hard to take. However, I am done with chemo for now. Through the next few months, I could let my body heal and relax and pray that the cancer is gone!

Coming into Canada Day Weekend, I need be patient with the chemo drugs slowly leaving my body that will be heaven, but it is a day to day healing that takes a number of weeks and for some months. For others the nerve damage is permanent. I was booked for another scan. This time of my upper chest and abdomen. So, praying that the doctors didn't suspect anything in my abdomen, I went in full of piss and vinegar, teasing the radiology tech by telling him that I am always happy to see someone with less hair than I have.

I kept my appointment with the oncologist, very anxious to find the results of the scan. I was pretty nervous and arrived at least ten minutes early. An hour and a half later I was near out of my mind. If I have a long wait for anything I assume the worst. Finally, in he came and he sat down and opened my file.

"Actually," he said, "I didn't need to see you today. Your scan looks good, so, at least for now, you can go on with your life without treatments. The radiation and chemmo treatments have shrunk the tumors all is dormant right now and we must take one day at a time. I am not saying that cancer won't return, but for now, all is well."

Tears were waiting to escape and I hugged my daughter in law and I was so relieved that I went into the chemmo room and cried as I told the angels that with any luck, they wouldn't have to put up with me again, and that my scan looked good. They gave me a survivor angel pin and I got hugs from everyone, what a day!

CHAPTER SEVEN

Courage

Inner messages telling me
over and over again,
don't give up, stay strong;
don't look back, keep going,
head up, shoulders straight,
one step at a time
climbing slowly, steadily
for you can and will
in your own time,
in your own way
conquer that mountain,
and when you do
you will no longer
be afraid for you are strong
strong like bull!

Two weeks into August and I am finally getting a
tiny bit of my energy back. Feeling a little better and apart
from the nerve pain, I am sleeping well, my appetite is
coming back, my memory is well - o.k. not being too swift
on returning. Anything to do with my brain or lack of same

will take a while longer. I always loved the lyric, "You may think I'm crazy, but it keeps me from going insane."

I am having a problem with standing up and then taking a dizzy spell. Last night I got up to pee and that definite feeling of going down hit me. The world went black. Down I went full weight with my face hitting the corner of the bedside table.

I woke to people around me but I was in a deep fog and didn't even want to open my eyes. In my mind, I wondered if I had died. I have no idea what it feels like and I thought after fighting a good fight, (I was aware of a little sob that found its way out of my throat). Well by Jesus, I may not have beat it yet, but I sure gave it a good ass kicking. The next thing I remember was someone saying, "Sue, Sue, come on wake up now, you are in the hospital, do you remember passing out?"

I felt really nice and warm, and comfy, like being in Grammy's bed when I was little. Then, in they came again. They stuck me with a needle and flicked at my toes, even stuck something in my heel, but would they never learn that I just wanted to sleep! Ah, alone at last, until just a bit later, I could again hear people in the room.

Someone was tapping on my right hand. Steve got right in my face and said "O.K., Mom, you have to quit with the sleeping thing, come on wake up for Christ sake! If you don't soon open your eyes, they will take you down to the morgue and down there, it's cold like hell after the fire went out!"

"Mom, Mom?"

Well, if I have to wake up, I guess I have to. " There, my eyes are open, are you happy now? What happened, did I pass out?"

"You had one of your infamous mini strokes. You should see your face, I don't know what you hit on the way down, but you have two black eyes, and a huge bump on your forehead. They kept you sedated so you would stay asleep until they could determine if there was any brain damage. Yea, I know you can't damage something that don't exist. They will take you for another scan and then I can take you home. Don't you ever damned well do that again, you had me thinking you were checking out!"

"Oh, come on, why would I go thru that huge surgery and all those treatments and then just die?" I chuckled?

"You know me, too full of piss and vinegar to do anything like that!"

About two weeks later, I was feeling much better and walking around the supermarket, of course with a cart to keep me steady on my feet. So far it had been a hot, hot summer and every time I wore the wig, I would sweat and itch so most of the time I wore a cap.

It was touch and go without feeling weak or dizzy, but now that more and more of the chemo drugs are finding their way out of my system, I have regained a bit of strength And much more energy. I can even crank myself on to make a list of what I need from the store and away I go. I finally care about my nutrition and weight and all that important stuff (well, somewhat and for at least a week). I pushed that little cart around the supermarket like a pro, trying not to look wonkey and clumsy on my feet, which are numb from the ankle down and keep getting in my way.

I keep trying to ignore the numbness in my hands which only bugs me when I am painting, typing, writing

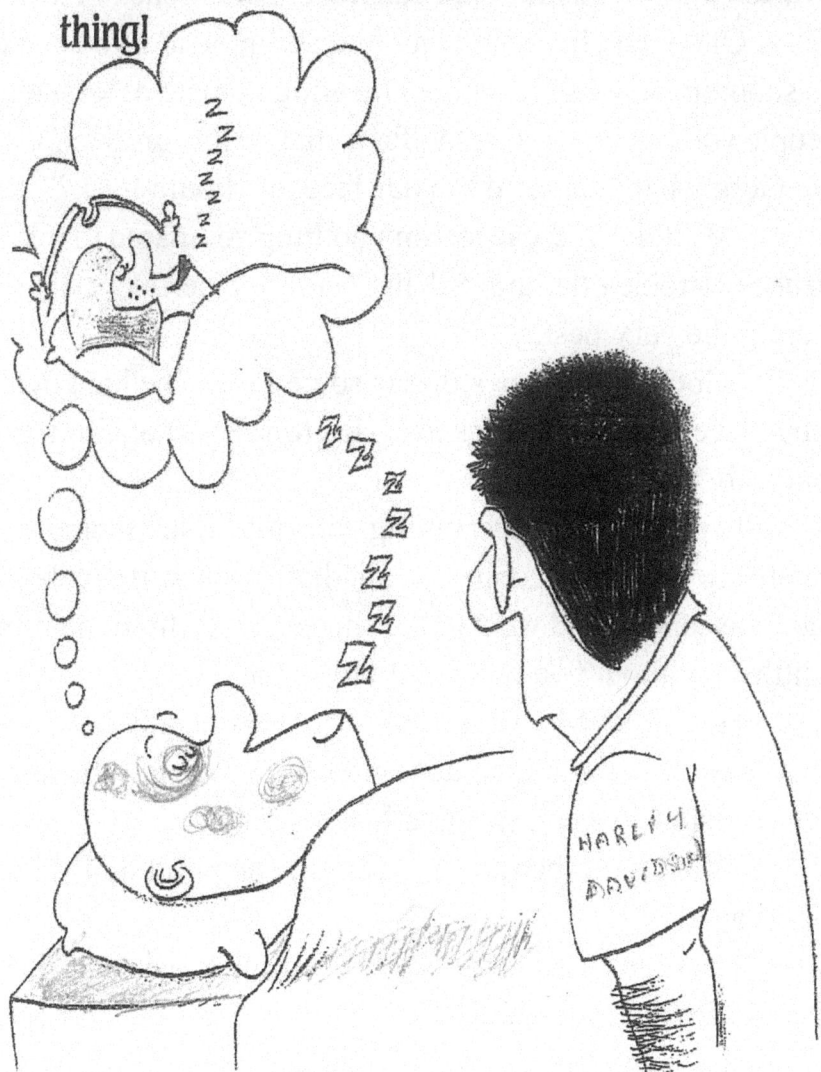

anything by hand. I print everything in caps now and have mastered that quite well, and I am improvising with anything that requires feeling in my fingers. (Sorry, Granny, up in heaven, no after all your hours of patiently teaching me how to curse at frustration, I can no longer crochet, or knit.

Of course, in a small city like Summerside, you can't go shopping anywhere without meeting up with at least ten people you know, so you stop for a chat, "How are you? Oh my God, what happened to your face, or should I ask?"

"Well, I guess cancer ain't nothing compared to mini strokes. I took one and fell flat on my face. Now, I am feeling the very best, you?"

"Good, good, boys that is some face. The hangover must have been some wicked . Nice to see you again dear, take care".

I picked up everything on my list, including blueberries and broccoli and all that good stuff to help fight the cancer, and went to the checkouts. Behind me was a little boy about five or six with his Mom.

He asked Mom "is that a man or a lady"? Mom answered "I think it is a lady and she is wearing that cap because she has been sick and lost her hair".

"Where did her hair go, couldn't she find it? I think she is an alien."

I couldn't resist the urge! With my black and blue face, I turned around and lifted my cap - winking at mom, I said "I am an alien!"

Well sir, the look on his face was priceless. His eyes were the size of saucers. He said "Oh wow! Holy crap, you are"!

I am an Alien!

The gal at the checkout, a student, started laughing. She laughed so much she got the hiccups and that got me laughing again. By the time I paid for my groceries, the people around us were all laughing and wondering what the hell was going on. So, away I went next door to buy an eight pack of Blue. There stocking the shelves was another old friend. He said "How are you doing, Sue?"

"Well, Vincent, I'm some handsome, but I feel great, yourself?"

"To tell the truth, I didn't see you in for a while, kind of got worried about you."

"Thanks bud, for your concern, I'm doing fine, just waiting for the bruises to heal and the hair to grow. If I am not in next week, dial 911, I could have fallen down again and couldn't get up, at my age, who knows? That would likely happen in front of the fridge while I was going for another beer. If you don't see me for a long time, that means I have quit drinking which would really be bad news - I'd be either dead or back on chemmo!"

I put my groceries and beer in the car and thought about how good it felt just to get out and do normal everyday things like shopping, talking to my old friends and have the energy to lug the bags into the trailer when I got home. By the time I got them in, I was dragging ass and still had to put them away, so I sat down for a few minutes until I caught my breath and decided to tackle the job at hand. I was so weak, I felt like my legs would collapse so I put the milk in the fridge, meat in the freezer and went to lay down for an hour.

So my recovery went, day by day a little stronger with a little more energy. If I could just get rid of the nerve pain, I would be out dancing, but that is another story.

A few days later I was sitting on the edge of my bed in shorts and T shirt examining my numb feet. They felt foreign to me as if they weren't my feet, it was the strangest feeling. I said to myself, "Self, your feet are attached to your legs, which are attached to your ars, they have to be yours". They still looked like feet I had never seen before, but one thing about numb feet, the spurs and corns and crooked toes don't hurt anymore.

It is the middle of August, 2013 and for the first time in three years, bit by bit, I am cutting my own grass. I am doing about ten by ten feet and then going in out of the sun to rest. I am not sure how far I will get, but at least I am trying and this should give me back some strength in my arms. On this day, I only got one square done, but as I said to myself, I said "self, tomorrow is another day, and that is the way life is."

Next day my neighbour Brenda, God love her, cut the rest of my yard and trimmed around the flowers and trees. She spent pretty well the whole day, I was so thankful, as my strength and energy are still not good.

Little by little, my sense of smell and taste are coming back, I can't say my memory is any better but then, if I have to tell the truth, it never was good, but at least now, I can have a normal pee!

I try to get out of the house every day. Even just to take Maggie for a walk or go for a drive. I am trying to get interested in things again, like painting and writing, but my finger tips are numb, so you can guess how many times spell check kicks in, and how many paintings I have given up on. Also, I need to beg, steal or borrow tons of energy before I can become me again. Also in August, Grandma Mac, Jean, my "other mother" who loves me like one of her own, came for a visit. Last summer I was pretty sick, she told me that she was afraid that I would die. So she promised me that this summer if all went well, she would come for three or four weeks. Ha, ha, I fooled her, she had promised and I am still alive and kicking ass. Well sir, we had a lot of laughs. She wanted her hair "done". I where I have only just a little show of fuzzies for hair, she is almost ninety, with lovely thick white hair. She asked me to stop in at the hairdresser at the top of our street, and go in ask if they did the old fashioned wash and set on rollers, and of course, "how much"? So in I went and asked the question.

The gal at the counter said "we don't have rollers that small, hon, but for you, we could order some in." I finally figured out what all the laughter was about, I had left my cap in the car.

It was a great visit for both of us. I took Mother up to the mall and introduced her to Danny and others in the old fart's club, no one asked her for a date, but then she is probably fifteen or twenty years older than them although she looks about sixty. Mother beat me every time at crib except for the couple of times she let me win, and then she tried to teach me how to play double solitaire. Being a slow learner, I kept blaming chemo brain on all my mistakes. We went to the Casino and I got the laugh this time, I won a few bucks and she lost a few! Although feeding twenty dollar bills into a machine that will chew them up and make them disappear isn't really something to laugh at, it feels so good to get out and have fun!

Cancer has taken away my house, but it can't take away my feelings of home. As our home on earth is only temporary, so a house is only a shelter and home is where we feel we belong. It has taken away my savings, retirement plan, pretty well every item of value I ever owned, but it can't take away the value of my life! The fact that I was here, that I raised my children, painted my paintings, wrote my stories, dreamed my dreams, took care of and helped people who could not help themselves brought joy, love and laughter to their lives and showed them that this world does care about them. All of this amounts to all I wanted in my life.

There is nothing funny about cancer, but it can be laughed at. It will never take away my sense of humor and ability to laugh even when I am the only one thinking it is funny.

It has made me stumble with weakness, but can't take away my fight and strength, hope and belief. Even at the most painful and depressing of times, hope and faith were always there for me. Cancer has given me great respect for other who are fighting and for the wonderful caring people who work and volunteer in Cancer Centers, God bless them all!

Now, at the end of September, the leaves are turning and the nights are getting chilly. I have a follow up appointment next week. My fingers and feet are still numb and painful at times. I have the same old constant pain in my temples, my right eye has blurred vision and I have a nagging cough that won't go away.

What if? Well what if? If it is back again, I will fight it again and again and again. There is no truce, no saying uncle with cancer, it takes no prisoners. It is either you win or you loose, and by God I will win!! Pretty gutsie for a good looking old broad with one ugly tit!

How long do I have? I don't know and I don't want to know. How long do you have? We will all leave this life sooner or later and only God decides when. I will keep going with or without cancer as long as I can.

I now have a new person to take care of. David, a delightful disabled fella who loves Elvis and knows every lyric to every song written from 1950 on. I swear he has a photo memory. It was heartbreaking for his parents to come to the realization that that they could no longer take care of him. He needs a good loving home, care, acceptance and respect for who he is. I give him that care it is what God meant me to do.

There is so much depth in knowing faith. It is an awareness of something greater than us, something to which we are connected. As long as there is a day and night, winter and summer, spring and fall, we will continue to dream, to hope and to believe that with each season we will be renewed as part of that cycle and that our dreams and our passions become the wind that fills our sails.

My cat remains the same pain in the ass. He still loves to bring his Mam a freshly killed treat. Sometimes it is up on my pillow when I open my eyes and sometimes he just drops it into my slipper. At six in the morning just slipping my foot into it is pure torture. He is what he is, a lovable beast, that is what cats are all about! Maggie is still the most beautiful loving little dog on earth. If I die before she does, I can think of fifty people who would take her and love her even beyond her death. I was talking to my sister Jean on the phone today and telling her about meeting up with an old friend on Saturday who said " Boys oh boys, you look good, how do you keep going?"

"Well, thank you," I replied. "at my age, a positive attitude will keep a smile on your face, you keep putting one foot ahead of the other, praying with each step that you don't trip and break a hip! But beyond that, you must have faith and hope, and always remember, don't trust a fart!"

Jean said "Oh Susie, you always were two bricks short of a load".

I replied, "Yes, dear, but on the bright side, two bricks short is better than three or four bricks short, now that would be a problem- love you!"

P.S. Hey, girls, I am still one hot Grandma! I don't think about the ugly tit anymore and - this year, SHORT HAIR IS IN!!

END

No, not that
side, this side!